Praise for *Seed to Table*

"Luay has an enormous amount of knowledge on growing beautiful produce. Beyond his knowledge, his love and dedication to bringing vegetables to life are unparalleled. This book is an interesting and fantastic combination of simple and tasty recipes, along with an approachable DIY guide to becoming a home gardener."

—**Afrim Pristine**, internationally renowned maître fromager of the Cheese Boutique, Food Network TV host, and author of *For the Love of Cheese*: *Recipes and Wisdom from the Cheese Boutique*

"*Seed to Table* is a fantastic, robust guide that will help you achieve the garden-to-table lifestyle you've always craved. From quick growing tips and in-depth gardening techniques to drool-worthy recipes to use or preserve your homegrown bounty—Luay has covered it all!"

—**Deanna Talerico**, garden expert, blogger, and founder of *Homestead and Chill*

"Luay makes growing your own food, even if just a small amount, into an achievable endeavor. Combining his expert growing advice with detailed crop guides and delicious, creative recipes, this book contains everything you could possibly need to know to enjoy fresh meals straight from the garden."

—**Niki Irving** of Flourish Flower Farm, flower farmer, florist, and author of *Growing Flowers*

Seed to Table

Seed to Table

A Seasonal Guide to Organically Growing, Cooking, and Preserving Food at Home

Luay Ghafari

yellow pear  press

CORAL GABLES

For permission requests, please contact the publisher at:
Mango Publishing Group
2850 S Douglas Road, 2nd Floor
Coral Gables, FL 33134 USA
info@mango.bz

For special orders, quantity sales, course adoptions and corporate sales, please email the publisher at sales@mango.bz. For trade and wholesale sales, please contact Ingram Publisher Services at customer.service@ingramcontent.com or +1.800.509.4887.

Seed to Table: A Seasonal Guide to Organically Growing, Cooking, and Preserving Food at Home

Library of Congress Cataloging-in-Publication number: 2022951369
ISBN: (print) 978-1-68481-162-5, (ebook) 978-1-68481-163-2
BISAC category code: GAR025000, GARDENING / Vegetables

Printed in China

For my mother and father. Your sacrifices, love, and perseverance made me the man I am today.

Table of Contents

Foreword

My dad had rows and rows of raspberries planted in the huge garden of our childhood home. During the hot summers and golden fall seasons, the bushes would be heavy with jammy berries that tasted like sunlight. In between and alongside the rows, there was chard, tomatoes, basil, kale, cucumbers, romaine, and more. The first "job" that my brother and I shared was picking half-pints of those berries that would be sold at our family's produce store.

It sounds so idyllic and wholesome, but truthfully, I could not stand doing the job! It was hot and dirty, there were bees everywhere, and my parents always did a once-over of every row that I picked from because I missed so many berries. We would get two dollars for every half-pint, I don't think I ever made more than twenty dollars in a single summer. I just wanted to be inside working at the store's cash register or at home reading *Seventeen* magazine parked under an air conditioning vent.

I only began to cultivate an appreciation for everything that went into those raspberries when I moved to Toronto after high school. My city-dwelling student lifestyle had me eating mostly bagels and pasta, chugging coffee, and practically living at the library. When I came home on weekends, my main priorities were getting some fresh air and actually eating vegetables.

My gratitude deepened even further a few years later when I decided to go vegan, enroll in a nutritional culinary program, work in restaurants, and volunteer at a local food bank–all at the same time. I quickly realized that my upbringing around seasonal food put me in a unique position to find fulfillment in all of these new endeavors.

When I started cooking new and exciting plant-based meals for myself that were heavy on local produce, I felt a level of energy and vitality that I hadn't experienced before. That excitement fed my hunger to learn more about this lifestyle and led me to ask myself how I could inspire others. Everything that I was learning in culinary school, at work, and at the food bank was propelling me forward with new motivation every week.

That period of my life circled around a central theme of local, feel-good food. My instructors at school always found ways to bring discussions of seasonality to our cooking labs. I was lucky enough to work for one of Canada's most prominent farm-to-table chefs. At the food bank, we were also planting community gardens with children in after-school education programs. I would grab my weekly produce at a farmer's market that

I passed on the way home after a day of classes. There was a synergy in how the learning began to come together with all of these experiences.

Years later when I started my cooking blog and settled into a home of my own for the first time, growing our food was top of mind. Unlike those raspberry picking days, the dirt, hot temperatures, and presence of insects did not deter me. Sharing photos of my extremely beginner efforts at vegetable gardening alongside the recipes on my blog was important to me. It's all about connection! If I could inspire folks to try growing their own herbs or tomatoes, and that in turn inspired them to cook more, I felt like I had accomplished something huge.

I still feel the same way now, several years later. Connecting the dots of sometimes homegrown, always seasonal, and deeply nourishing food keeps me and my readers going. Seeing this movement of deeper connection grow across the internet, social media, and beautiful books like this one inspires me all over again.

—Laura Wright, cookbook author, recipe developer, and creator of *The First Mess*

Farm Life, circa 1988

First CSA, 2006

Montreal, 2006

George Brown College

George Brown College

Toronto, 2014

Introduction

For years, my interest in food was focused predominantly on cooking. I had very little interest in what happened before my ingredients made their way to my local market or grocery store. That changed in 2009 when I began participating in a CSA (community supported agriculture) program. It was almost as if I had this epiphany, an awakening of sorts. I still remember the name of the farmer, André Samson, from Farnham, Québec. That first CSA box was somewhat strange: organic fruits and vegetables that looked nothing like the perfectly shaped, unblemished produce we're all used to seeing at the store. I will admit that it took me some time to deprogram myself and appreciate the beauty in the unique. But the vegetables tasted great, and I was hooked. We got into the car and drove to Jean-Talon Market, where I purchased my first ever tomato, cucumber, and basil seedlings. For the next three years, I learned as much as I could about urban agriculture and container gardens.

After moving to Toronto in 2013, I enrolled in the culinary arts program at George Brown College. I did not intend to make culinary arts a career path but wanted to expose myself to new techniques and practices and learn from my peers. It was this experience that cemented for me the desire to focus on seasonality and self-sufficiency. Up until this point, I was living exclusively in condos with small balconies. I was yearning for more space. It was not until we purchased our first house with a backyard that my imagination took off—there were so many possibilities. Though small, my urban garden held lots of potential.

It was on a particularly tough and exhausting business trip in 2018 that I decided to launch Urban Farm and Kitchen, my gardening, cooking, and lifestyle blog. In an instant, I purchased the domain name and created my first logo. Soon after, I announced it to my Instagram followers. My vision was at first not quite clear, but I knew that long term, I would be working toward a garden-to-table initiative or business of some sort. My passion for gardening and seasonal cooking could not remain a hobby forever. I wanted more.

It has been a wonderful journey filled with challenges and triumphs. In many ways, I did it on my own, trying, failing, adjusting, adapting, perfecting. Persevering through failure is not a trait that everyone possesses. Unfortunately, failure in the garden can lead to a sense of hopelessness that can push new gardeners to give up. I don't want that for anyone. There is peace in growing a garden. There is a sense of optimism and wonder, a connection with nature that centers us and makes us appreciate the world around us. My hope is that more and more people experience this joy.

Writing this book has been a joy as well. In many ways, it has given me the opportunity to think back and truly appreciate my journey and how I became the person I am today. I hope that this book and the experiences, knowledge, and ideas within it will inspire you and support you in crafting and executing your own garden-to-table vision.

How to Use This Book

Is this a cookbook? Or is it a gardening book? Well, it's both. When conceptualizing this book, I simply couldn't divorce the act of cooking the food from the act of growing it. I wrote this book in a way that encourages you to think about the entire life cycle, from seed to plant to table.

- Chapter 1 dives deeper into my garden-to-table philosophy and includes practical advice to help you plan an abundant garden and become more self-sufficient in the process.

- In Chapter 2, I distill my 10+ years of edible gardening knowledge into 21 easy-to-read crop guides, full of tips, tricks, and recommendations. If you encounter unfamiliar terminology, refer to the glossary of common terms at the back of this book.

- Chapter 3 offers you recipes that I hope will inspire you to grow more of what you like to eat. After all, what's the point of growing abundant fruits and vegetables if we don't transform them into delectable dishes to enjoy and share?

- Chapters 4 through 10 cover the technical aspects of garden planning, growing techniques, fundamentals of soil health, seed starting, garden maintenance, and more.

Throughout the book, you will find QR codes that will take you to my website, where I provide additional information, context, specialized techniques, related content, or advice in the form of a short instructional video or blog post. To view the digital content, simply hover your phone camera over the QR code and click on the link. Alternatively, in the back of the book, you will find a list of the pages with QR codes along with the specific website URLs so that you can navigate via your computer's web browser in case you do not have access to a smartphone.

Why don't you go ahead and scan the first QR code now?

Chapter 1

Garden-to-Table

Farm-to-table, a concept that has been around for some time, is defined as a social movement that promotes serving locally sourced or locally grown food at restaurants and school cafeterias. Sometimes a restaurant will specify a radius (e.g., 100-mile farm-to-table), or a list of suppliers is made available to the public.

Garden-to-table borrows from the farm-to-table movement and shrinks that radius down to one's own backyard. You are the chef, the farmer, and the consumer. You are invested in every step of the process, from the planning of your garden to planting, maintaining, harvesting, cooking, preserving, composting, and more.

Garden-to-table isn't just a movement, but truly a way of life. It fosters a closer connection with nature and the soil that feeds us all. It helped me embrace the seasonality of food, achieve a greater level of self-sufficiency, and build community in the process.

A Matter of Taste

Ask any gardener and they will tell you, without a shadow of a doubt, that a vine-ripened tomato is the stuff dreams are made of. There is simply no comparison to store-bought. Many of the fruits available for purchase at your local grocery stores have not been harvested at peak ripeness. Tomatoes, for example, are harvested prematurely and undergo forced ripening through ethylene gas exposure. Conversely, kale harvested in the summer months can be bitter and unappetizing. The same applies to lettuce and other greens as they get exposed to summer heat and begin to bolt (go to flower). Seasonality matters.

The growing requirements of various crops differ greatly. Some like it hot, others not so much. There are other nuances to this, but for the sake of simplicity, in this book, I categorize crops as either cool-weather or warm-weather crops. Cool-weather crops include spring and fall/winter favorites like arugula, lettuce, kale, Asian greens, and peas. Warm-weather crops include heat lovers like tomatoes, peppers, eggplants, squash, and beans.

This categorization also translates over to flavor. Cool-weather crops thrive in the colder seasons and taste best when harvested under cooler conditions. Warm-weather crops thrive in the heat of summer and are typically in season (at their peak) in the summer months. This is a general rule of thumb, and there are of course exceptions, depending on the region and climate. Chapter 4 covers the topic of growing zones and microclimates in more detail.

For me, walking into my garden with a basket in hand and harvesting homegrown fruits and vegetables at peak ripeness is what I love about having a garden. Taking what my garden provides and creating seasonal recipes is what garden-to-table living is all about.

LAVENDER CALENDULA CALENDULA

GINGER TURMERIC '21 SAGE

KOREAN CHILI AI DRAGON ALEPPO SMOKED PEPPER REZHA M. CAYENNE AJI PINE SRP OREGANO/THYME

On the Road to Self-Sufficiency

Self-sufficiency and gardening are often linked. Being able to grow your own sustenance is in and of itself an act of self-sufficiency. Although I'm a strong proponent of growing food, I can firmly and confidently say that I don't have the ability to become completely self-sufficient. Not only is this difficult to achieve where I live, but it would also make for a pretty boring existence. We are incredibly lucky to live in a time where we have access to both local and foreign produce, products, and ingredients to meet a range of cultural and dietary needs throughout the year.

Take one look at your fridge and pantry and you'll know right away that growing 100% of your food is probably not a realistic goal. In fact, I would argue that setting a 100% self-sufficiency goal can be counterproductive. Are you prepared to give up on difficult or impossible to grow staples from your diet? Can you say goodbye to chocolate forever because cacao trees can't grow in your climate? What about olive oil? How about lemons? On the flip side, are you prepared to devote your entire garden to growing pinto beans because your family enjoys refried beans twice a week? Balance is key.

Becoming more self-sufficient requires us to understand and appreciate our limitations—limitations due to climate, location, experience, processing power, and more. I prefer to think of self-sufficiency as a journey of small, tangible steps that help us eat more locally and reduce our dependency on others while still enjoying our lives.

When deciding what to grow in my garden, I usually ask myself the following questions:

- **Do I need to grow it?** One example is corn. Can I grow it? I certainly can. However, it can take up a considerable amount of space, and the yields per square foot are low. I will come back to this example later on in this book.

- **Will it thrive in my garden?** This is such an important question that is often overlooked. Different crops have different requirements. There's really little point in using up precious growing space on a crop that won't thrive, mature, or produce in your climate or location.

- **Will it save me money?** In my limited space, I prefer to focus on high-value crops like heirloom tomatoes, eggplants, and peppers. An heirloom tomato can cost upwards of $5 a pound at the market. Growing my own is both economical and rewarding.

- **Do I even like it?** We have all fallen into the trap of growing something that ends up tasting, shall we say, not as we had anticipated. One example is celery. Homegrown celery, in my experience, tastes nothing like what we are typically used to.

- **Can I preserve it?** Preserving the harvest must be part of your overall self-sufficiency and garden-to-table strategy. Growing crops that can easily be dehydrated, canned, frozen, pickled, fermented, and processed in several ways will go a long way in helping you become more self-sufficient.

- **How versatile is it?** Variety is the spice of life. Growing crops that can be transformed into a wide range of dishes will keep you engaged and interested.

Many gardeners look to seed catalogs for inspiration. With so many colors, textures, and varieties available, you can really get lost in it all. My approach is a little different. I pull inspiration from cookbooks, restaurants, and my favorite chefs. I look at what they are doing, what resonates with me, and what is new and compelling. I consider what I want to preserve and enjoy in the winter months. I think about what I want to share with my friends, family, and community. A lot goes into the planning process, and I encourage you to refer to Chapter 4 for a more in-depth discussion on planning your dream garden.

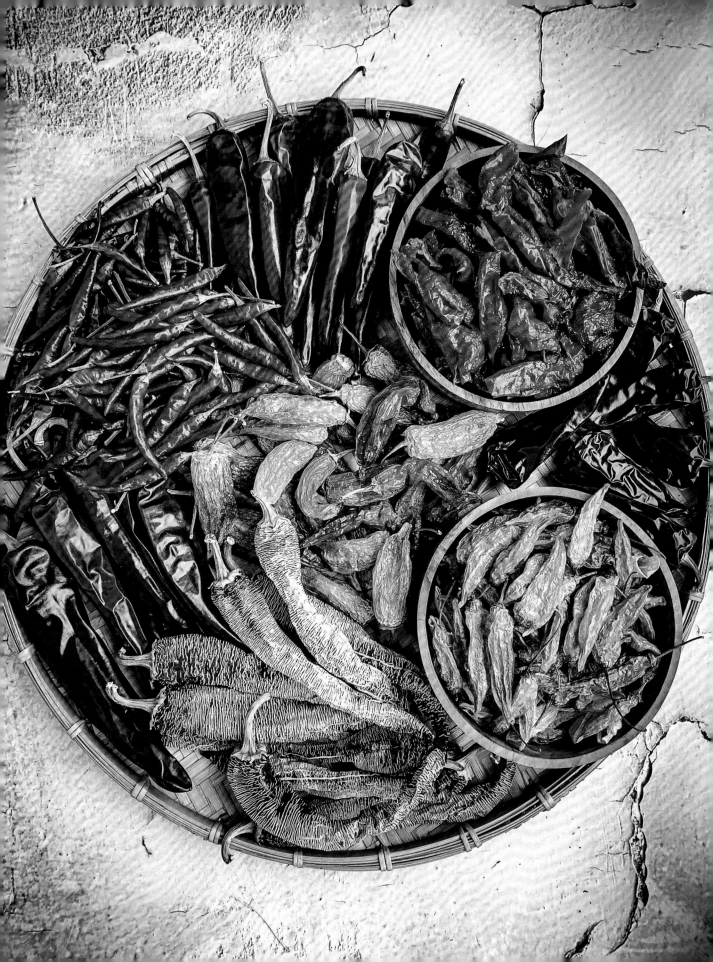

A Communal Act

Growing a garden is a communal act. It may not seem like it when you are tending to your crops, alone with your thoughts. But I promise you, your neighbors are looking. They are watching you work the soil, inspect your plants, and harvest the fruits of your labor. You are inspiring friends and family. You are actively taking a role in the beautification of your neighborhood, no matter how big or small your space may be. You are building community.

I cannot tell you how many conversations I have struck up with neighbors, both at home and at my allotment garden. Growing food is universal. Language barriers topple in an instant. Gardeners may seem stuck in their ways, but in my experience, most are curious and willing to learn from fellow growers. Gardeners are givers, sharing seeds, knowledge, expertise, support, encouragement, and of course, harvests with one another.

If growing food is universal, eating food is what connects us all. Most if not all of the world's cultures have some sort of communal dining concept where food is shared and enjoyed among friends and family. Examples include Italian antipasto, Middle Eastern mezze, Spanish tapas, Chinese dim sum, Swiss fondue, and Swedish smörgåsbord. The garden-to-table movement embraces communal dining, and I for one love nothing more than to dine outside on a warm summer evening with friends, wine, and delicious food prepared using fresh ingredients harvested right from that very garden. It's intentional, meaningful, and magical.

Chapter 2

Crop Guides

This chapter will focus on high-yield crops that perform well in small spaces and urban and suburban gardens, as well as balconies and terraces. After years of trials filled with successes and some failures, I've concluded that some crops are simply not worth growing if space is at a premium. One such crop is maize (corn). In my opinion, corn is not a suitable crop for home gardeners, especially beginners. Growing it organically can be difficult from a pest and disease mitigation perspective. In addition, it is not high-yield and requires a considerable amount of space. I prefer to rely on my local corn farmers for all my corn needs in late summer and early fall.

These 21 crop guides include a brief description of the crop and my reasons for growing it, along with information on its growth pattern, growing difficulty, and suitability for small spaces and balconies, as well as common issues that an organic gardener might face. Tips on growing, maintaining, harvesting, and storing are also included. I've also decided to share some of my favorite varietals to help guide you in your seed selection process. These crop guides are meant to be an overview. For specific information, refer to the technical information laid out in Chapters 4 through 10.

If you encounter terminology that sounds unfamiliar to you, I encourage you to refer to the glossary of common terms at the back of this book.

Cool-Weather Crops

Radish

[Raphanus raphanistrum subsp. sativus.]

The humble radish is anything but humble. It can be consumed raw, fermented, pickled, or even roasted. Available in an array of colors and shapes, radishes add a crunchy punch to salads, tacos, kimchi, and more. The greens are also edible and can be stir-fried or used to make a pungent pesto. Considered a cool-weather crop, radishes thrive in mild climates in spring, fall, and winter. They generally do not appreciate summer heat and will bolt (go to flower). Broadly speaking, radishes are categorized either as Spring (or European) or Winter radishes. Spring radishes are those that are quick to mature, typically in 25–40 days. These include common varieties like French Breakfast, Sora, and Easter Egg (not quite a variety, but a collection of colorful varieties). Winter radishes are typically larger and take much longer to mature. They include varieties like Daikon and Black Spanish.

They are one of the first seeds to go into the ground and one of the first crops to be harvested. After a long winter, there's nothing more rewarding than pulling something colorful and delicious from my garden.

Growth pattern: Like other root crops, radishes should be directly sown. They germinate and grow quickly under the right conditions, and therefore there is no need to start them indoors. Starting them indoors and transplanting them will disturb the root structure and could yield deformed roots. Spring varieties will remain quite compact and can even be sown in clusters. Spring radish foliage typically stays short. Winter varieties can grow quite large, with foliage that spreads over 12" (30cm).

Growing difficulty level: Easy. This is one crop I recommend planting with your kids. Because of how quickly the radishes grow, children will remain engaged in the process.

Suitability for small spaces and balconies: Spring or European varieties are recommended for small spaces as they have shallow roots. They can be planted in window box planters, grow bags, and other containers.

Common issues: Slugs, irregular roots, root damage from insect bites.

Tips for success:

- As soon as the soil is workable in the spring, begin direct sowing. If you live in a region with mild winters, consider growing radishes throughout your cool season. Some seed suppliers will provide optimal soil temperature germination guidelines.

- Radishes should be planted in succession to avoid a glut and ensure constant harvesting over several weeks. Refer to the succession planting discussion in Chapter 5.

How to maintain healthy plants: Because of how quickly they grow, there isn't much maintenance required. If you sowed your seeds heavily, you may want to consider thinning (strategically pulling seedlings) to provide enough space for others to grow to maturity. Consult the seed packet for spacing information.

When and how to harvest: You'll know that the radish is ready to be harvested when its shoulders are visible and you can see that the root has plumped up. If you wait too long to harvest, the root may become pithy and unappetizing. The best way to know they are ready and tasty? Gently pull one out, wash, and sample.

Storage tips: I recommend you only harvest what you need for a given recipe or meal. However, if you must harvest a large quantity for storage, wrap radishes, with their taproots and greens attached, in moist paper towels and place them in a reusable plastic bag or container. Refrigerate until needed. They will keep for several days this way. Check on them regularly, and if the greens begin to turn mushy, clean the radishes and preserve them.

Favorite and recommended varieties:

- **Zlata:** A golden globe variety that is somewhat heat-tolerant and can withstand a late spring warmup.

- **French Breakfast:** A classic elongated bi-color radish. A must grow in my opinion.

- **Easter Egg:** A standard rainbow mix of radishes that offers a fun, easy way to grow a rainbow without worrying about specific varieties.

Recipes:

- Burrata and Spring Pesto Toast (Page 131)
- Herbaceous Lettuce and Radish Salad (Page 150)
- Refrigerator Pickles, 7 Ways (Page 205)

Lettuce

[Lactuca sativa]

This quintessential leafy vegetable might just be one of the most common vegetables in the world. The textures, flavors, and colors of homegrown lettuce simply cannot be found at the grocery store. The ability to harvest a crispy head of romaine from my garden minutes before making a Caesar salad is a simple pleasure that I relish year after year.

Growth pattern: Lettuce is a cool-weather crop that can be cultivated in one of two ways. It may be grown as head lettuce, where a single seed is allowed to mature to form a single head of lettuce (what you would traditionally see in the produce aisle). Alternatively, lettuce may be cultivated as baby greens, where many seeds are sown closely together and harvested when the leaves are still young (what you see packaged as lettuce mixes or mesclun in bags or clear clamshell containers in the refrigerated section of your produce aisle).

Growing difficulty level: Easy. Lettuce can be directly sown outdoors or started indoors for transplanting.

Suitability for small spaces and balconies:
Lettuce is suitable for balconies and small gardens as it does not require any support and will reach maturity relatively quickly. It also has a shallow root structure, making it an ideal container crop.

Common issues: Cutworms, flea beetles, slugs, downy mildew.

Tips for success:

- For head lettuce: Seeds can be started indoors or in a greenhouse 4 weeks before being transplanted into the garden. Transplant seedlings outdoors when the soil is workable and overnight temps are at least 39°F/4°C. Follow the seed packet for specific instructions. Seeds can also be direct sown. However, starting seeds in advance gives you a head start on the growing season.

- For baby lettuce: Broadcast seeds densely when soil is workable in the spring and carefully sprinkle with enough soil or growing medium to achieve the correct planting depth specified on your seed packet, typically ¼" (5 mm).

- In regions where spring is short, consider growing heat-tolerant varieties.

- Growing lettuce in containers helps keep certain pests at bay.

- If you enjoy lettuce, consider succession planting to ensure an abundant and staggered harvest.

How to maintain healthy plants:

- From an aesthetic point of view, we want to avoid or minimize pest pressure. Consider using a row cover or insect barrier to protect your crop.

- As the weather warms up, lettuce will be prone to bolting (going to seed), which will render it bitter and unappetizing. On hot days, you may need to water your lettuce crop multiple times and/or consider using shade cloth.

When and how to harvest: Baby leaf lettuce can be harvested as needed, leaving the inner growth points untouched so that new leaves can continue to grow. Head lettuce is typically harvested when the head reaches the desired size. Take a sharp knife and run it along the soil line to detach the lettuce head from the root. Alternatively, you can remove outer leaves as needed while allowing the center to keep growing (this is best done with romaine-type lettuce). Lettuce should be harvested in the early morning or evening. To keep your lettuce crisp and prevent it from going limp, let it sit in cool water for 30 minutes before drying it off and storing it.

Storage tips:

- For baby lettuce, wash and spin dry. Store in a reusable, resealable plastic bag in the refrigerator. You can also store it in a container lined with paper towels. Your baby lettuce is now usable as is and doesn't require any further rinsing.

- For head lettuce, store in a reusable loose plastic bag lined with a paper towel to absorb any excess water left over from soaking. Keep the head intact to make it last longer in the fridge. When ready to use, break apart, wash, spin dry, and enjoy.

Favorite and recommended varieties:

- **Salanova:** Incredibly attractive and delicious head lettuce.
- **Coastal Star:** Heat tolerant Romaine-type.

Recipes:

- Herbaceous Lettuce and Radish Salad (Page 150)

Carrots

[Daucus carota subsp. sativus*]*

What we know as carrots today are domesticated forms of wild carrot (a.k.a. Queen Anne's Lace). The domesticated carrot has its roots in Central Asia, i.e., modern-day Iran and Afghanistan. Though most people know of orange carrots, there are in fact several varieties of white, yellow, red, and purple carrots to suit all tastes and preferences. Growing carrots in a home garden setting can be tricky if timing and conditions are not ideal. One of the most common complaints about homegrown carrots is that they taste soapy or piney. What gives carrots their flavor is a balance of sugars and terpenoids, volatile compounds which can often be described as smelling and tasting of pine, wood, or even turpentine. Young carrots develop terpenoids first, and if harvested too early, a carrot can taste bitter and soapy. As carrots mature, natural sugars develop through photosynthesis. These sugars are stored in the root. Carrots are cool-weather vegetables and perform best in regions with a prolonged cool growing season.

Pulling carrots from the ground is incredibly rewarding. It's also a surprise every time. Some of the most interesting varieties are not typically found at the store or market, so growing my own allows me to experiment with different colors and flavor profiles.

Growth pattern: Once a carrot seed germinates, it begins sending down a tap root, which will eventually swell and transform into the carrot root we all know. As carrots grow, their tops (greens) will bush out, protecting the soil below from the sun's rays and helping reduce evaporation. Carrots need moisture to grow. If you live in a region with low precipitation, hand watering might be required.

Growing difficulty level: Intermediate. They are not the easiest crop to grow, and it can be difficult to achieve uniform seed germination. However, once seeds germinate, the plants are generally fuss-free and require minimal maintenance.

Suitability for small spaces/balconies: Carrots are not considered a high-yield crop as they can take quite some time to mature. In a balcony or patio situation, you can grow smaller varieties in containers. Paris Market, a distinctive variety that grows in a round and stubby shape, is ideal for containers. If your preference is to grow standard varieties, a container that is at least 18" (45 cm) tall will be required.

Common issues: Carrot fly, wireworms, leaf blight.

Tips for success:

- If you live in a region with a short spring or fall, select varieties with a shorter number of days to maturity (DTM).

- Excess nitrogen in the soil will cause the carrots to grow bushier tops at the expense of the roots. Do not amend your carrot beds with nitrogen-rich compost or fertilizers.

- To ensure proper root formation, the soil must be loose and free of rocks and clumps of clay. If needed, incorporate some sand in the garden bed to help loosen it up and break apart any large masses of compacted soil.

- Heavily sow your carrot seeds by scattering them or by creating neat rows. Surface sow your seeds. Seeds need constant moisture to germinate. Water carefully so that the seeds do not wash away, and cover with a burlap sheet or other permeable material to keep the soil from moving and to prevent pests from digging in the bed.

How to maintain healthy plants: Thin your carrots by removing some of the immature plants in a row or patch to free up space for the rest so that they can grow to full size. You may need to repeat this process 2 or 3 times in a season. To thin, carefully pull out the immature carrot plant at the soil line while ensuring the neighboring plants are undisturbed. The thinning process can begin when the carrot tops are at least 5" (13 cm) tall.

When and how to harvest: Knowing when carrots are ready to harvest is tricky. One telltale sign is when their shoulders (the top of the carrot root where the greens are attached) are exposed above the soil line. Often the seed packet or supplier website will include information on the expected length and girth of a specific variety. Pull one carrot and see if the desired size has been achieved. If

not, you can let them continue to grow. There's no harm in harvesting young carrots, but bear in mind that they may not have developed their sweet flavor yet. If you leave them in the ground too long, they may become woody and their flavor may be compromised.

Storage tips: For short-term storage, gently wash, dry, and place in a reusable plastic bag in the refrigerator.

Favorite and recommended varieties:

- **Paris Market:** Ideal for small spaces and container growing.
- **Deep Purple F1:** Purple Imperator type (long and thin). Striking and beautiful to grow.
- **Napoli F1:** Quickly maturing Nantes type (shorter and stubbier than Imperator). A good all-around carrot variety.

Recipes:

- Sweet and Sour Roasted Carrots (Page 186)
- Refrigerator Pickle, 7 Ways (Page 205)
- Harvest Giardiniera (Page 209)

Arugula

[Eruca vesicaria]

Arugula (a.k.a. rocket, rucula, or roquette) is a cool-weather annual native to the Mediterranean that produces flavorful and tender greens from the same family as cabbage, kale, and horseradish (Brassicaceae). Delicious, spicy, peppery arugula leaves are a perfect addition to salad, pizza, pasta, and sandwiches. It grows rather quickly and is one of the earliest crops I can harvest in my spring garden.

Growth pattern: Arugula can be grown either for its tender baby leaves or allowed to mature. Baby arugula is typically planted densely like baby lettuce and harvested as a cut-and-come-again crop. Alternatively, it can be grown as individual plants for bunching that will mature with much larger leaves. Arugula grown for bunching tends to be much more pungent and is used in cooked preparations, while baby arugula is used in salads and other raw recipes. Arugula is a cool-weather crop and will bolt (go to flower) as temperatures rise. A telltale sign that your arugula is bolting and no longer delicious is the appearance of fuzz or little hairs on the stem.

Growing difficulty level: Easy.

Suitability for small spaces and balconies: Arugula grown as baby leaves works well in containers.

Common issues: Flea beetles, cabbage butterfly, downy mildew.

Tips for success:

- Arugula prefers to be directly sown. However, in regions where spring is short, consider starting arugula indoors 4 weeks before transplanting outside. This helps give you a head start.

- Succession plant arugula to ensure continuous harvests.

How to maintain healthy plants: Because it grows quickly and at a time when pest pressure is low, there isn't much maintenance required.

When and how to harvest: Harvest baby leaves as needed, leaving the inner growth points untouched so that new leaves can continue to grow.

Storage tips: Wash, thoroughly spin dry, and refrigerate in an airtight container or reusable bag.

Favorite and recommended varieties:

- **Astro:** Excellent all-around variety. It's not as peppery as other varieties, which makes it more suitable for picky eaters.
- **Red Dragon:** Striking green leaves with red veining.

Recipes:

- Spring Pesto (Page 163)
- Burrata and Spring Pesto Toast (Page 131)

Cabbage, Broccoli, and Cauliflower

[Brassica oleracea]

Cabbage (var. *capitata*), Broccoli (var. *italica*), and Cauliflower (var. *botrytis*) are cultivars of *Brassica oleracea*, which in its uncultivated form is Wild Mustard, native to Western Europe. Other cultivars of this species include Kale, Brussels Sprouts, Gai Lan, and Kohlrabi. This crop species is incredibly important to many cultures and countries around the world. The crunch you get from a homegrown cabbage is simply unparalleled. I typically grow rare or unique varieties that are not available at the farmers' market or grocery store.

Growth pattern: These brassicas grow no taller than 2' (60cm) but can spread up to 3' (90cm) wide depending on the variety. Compact varieties are recommended for urban and suburban gardens. These crucifers are considered cool-weather crops and do not perform well in the summer. Proper planning and timing are critical to a successful harvest.

Growing difficulty level: Difficult. In many ways, successfully growing brassicas is a badge of honor for home gardeners. They are finicky and require precise timing and growing conditions to thrive and produce. If seeds are started too early or there is a delay in transplanting, seedlings may bolt prematurely due to stress. If seedlings are transplanted too late, crops may not have enough time to mature before the weather warms up. That being said, if you try and fail, don't give up. Try again the following year and adjust your timing accordingly.

Suitability for small spaces and balconies: Not suitable. Although you can grow certain compact varieties of these crops in large containers, the yield is simply too low to make them worthwhile in my opinion.

Common issues: Cabbage white butterfly, flea beetles, slugs, powdery mildew, and damping off (in seedling stage).

Tips for success:

- Select varieties suitable for your region and climate. If you live in a region with a short spring, varieties that need a shorter number of days to maturity (DTM) will be ideal.

- Seeds must be started indoors or in a greenhouse 4–5 weeks before being transplanted into the garden. Transplant seedlings when the soil is workable and overnight temps are at least 39°F/4°C. Follow seed packet for timing instructions.

- Be prepared to cover your crops if necessary. A late freeze or an early heat wave may require deploying a frost barrier or shade cloth.

How to maintain healthy plants:

- The best way to ensure your brassicas thrive is to protect them from cabbage white butterflies. This is achieved by covering crops with an insect barrier or row cover to prevent the butterfly from laying eggs on the leaves in the first place.

- White cauliflower varieties require an additional blanching step to ensure they remain white and bright. Blanching is achieved by tying the outer leaves around the cauliflower head as it begins to form and securing them with string, clothespins, or even binder clips.

When and how to harvest: Cabbage will be ready to harvest when the head feels tight and has little to no give when squeezed. Broccoli should be harvested while the florets are still tight and before they begin to open and flower. Cauliflower should be harvested before the curds (the flower clusters) begin to separate. Broccoli and cauliflower plants may produce side shoots after the main head is harvested.

Storage tips: Store your harvested broccoli, cauliflower, and cabbage in large reusable plastic bags in your refrigerator. Broccoli and cauliflower heads can be separated into pieces and frozen for future use. Leftover cabbage can be shredded and turned into sauerkraut or frozen in individual reusable bags and added to soups.

Favorite and recommended varieties:

- **Tiara F1 Cabbage:** A compact hybrid that matures quickly. Ideal for small gardens and short cool seasons.
- **Graffiti F1 Cauliflower:** A stunning purple cauliflower that is a dream to watch grow.
- **Eastern Magic F1 Broccoli:** A reliable standard variety that was developed to resist stress.

Recipes:

- Roasted Cauliflower with Tahini and Salsa Macha (Page 189)
- Harvest Giardiniera (Page 209)

Kale and Collard Greens

[Brassica oleracea]

Bred for leaf growth, kale (var. *sabellica*) and collard greens (var. *viridis*) are cultivars of the same species as cabbage, broccoli, cauliflower, and brussels sprouts. I'm not the biggest fan of kale, and yet it's always growing and thriving in my garden. I find it architecturally interesting, and it looks beautiful in my urban garden. I use it in smoothies or as a substitute for spinach, in coleslaws, soups, and braises.

Growth pattern: Although they prefer cooler temperatures, spring-planted kale and collard greens can grow through the summer and into fall and even winter. In milder regions, they can be planted in the fall and continue to grow for months undeterred. As biennial crops, they will spend their first year focusing on producing leaves. In their second year, they will focus on reproducing and go to seed (bolting). I recommend starting with new seedlings every year to ensure abundant leafy harvests. Kale and collard greens can also be densely planted and harvested in baby leaf form to be consumed raw in salads, similarly to arugula and mesclun mixes.

Growing difficulty level: Easy. They are one of the easiest cultivars in the Brassica family to grow and thus are a great introduction to this diverse plant family for new gardeners.

Suitability for small spaces and balconies: Unlike their space-intensive cousins, kale and collard greens can grow well in containers and small spaces.

Common issues: Cabbage white butterfly, flea beetles, slugs, aphids, damping off (in seedling stage).

Tips for success:

- Seeds can be started indoors or in a greenhouse 4–5 weeks before being transplanted into the garden. Transplant seedlings when the soil is workable and overnight temps are at least 39°F/4°C. Follow seed packet for timing instructions. Seeds can also be directly sown. However, starting seeds in advance gives you a head start on the growing season.

- Be prepared to cover your crops if necessary. A late freeze or an early heat wave may require deploying a frost barrier or shade cloth.

How to maintain healthy plants:

- The best way to ensure that your kale and collard greens thrive is to protect them from cabbage white butterflies. Cover crops with an insect barrier or row cover to prevent the butterfly from laying eggs in the first place.

- Inspect the growing tips regularly for aphids as an aphid infestation can stunt plants and reduce output.

When and how to harvest: You may harvest leaves as needed, starting with the lower leaves first. Be mindful not to accidentally cut the growing tip as this will set your plant back significantly.

Storage tips: I recommend harvesting what you need for a given recipe or meal, but if you must harvest a large quantity, wrap leaves in a moist paper or cloth towel, place the bundle in a reusable plastic bag, and refrigerate.

Favorite and recommended varieties:

- **Scarlet Kale:** Ruffled purple leaves that add color and texture to your garden and your table.

- **Lacinato (Dino) Kale:** An Italian heirloom with greenish-blue leaves that resemble the skin of a dinosaur.

Recipes:

- Autumn Pesto (Page 165)
- Curried Lentils and Greens (Page 172)

Swiss Chard / Beetroot

[Beta vulgaris]

To the untrained eye, beetroots and Swiss chard are two distinct crops. However, they are both cultivars of the same plant species. Swiss chard (a.k.a. spinach beet) was bred for its juicy, succulent leaves. Beetroot (a.k.a. garden beet) was bred for big, sweet roots. Swiss chard adds color and an architectural aesthetic to the garden. Homegrown beetroots are simply divine, and their flavor is far superior to what is available at the grocery store or market.

Growth pattern: Beetroot and Swiss chard seeds are multigerm since they are technically a cluster of fused seeds that results in potentially multiple seedlings. Swiss chard is a biennial plant. It has a two-year life cycle in regions where winters are mild and it is allowed to overwinter. It will bolt (flower and set seed) in its second year. I recommend growing it as an annual because when it bolts, the leaves turn bitter and unappetizing. Beetroot will grow in very much the same way as Swiss chard. Under ideal conditions, the roots will begin to swell. Both are considered cool-weather crops and thrive in spring, fall, and mild winters. However, they can be quite heat-tolerant and may continue to grow and thrive through the summer months if well protected and shaded on particularly warm days. If the weather warms up before the roots begin to swell, the likelihood of beetroots bolting increases. Swiss chard leaves and stalks are edible, and so are beetroot greens.

Growing difficulty level: Easy.

Suitability for small spaces and balconies: Both beetroots and Swiss chard can be grown in containers and small spaces.

Common issues: Leaf miner, flea beetles, slugs, downy mildew, and damping off (seedling stage).

Tips for success: Both chard and beetroot seedlings are prone to damping off. When starting seeds indoors or in a greenhouse, make sure to water your cells or plugs from below. See Chapter 8.

How to maintain healthy plants: Because Swiss chard and beets are susceptible to leaf miner damage, it is advisable to cover them with an insect barrier or row cover. This prevents the fly from laying eggs on the underside of leaves in the first place.

When and how to harvest: Swiss chard can be harvested as needed by carefully snapping or pruning outer leaves. Regular harvesting will encourage the plants to send out fresh new leaves from the center of the plant. Beetroots can be harvested as needed when the roots reach the desired size.

Storage tips: I recommend harvesting what you need for a given recipe or meal, but if you must harvest a large quantity, wrap leaves in a moist paper or cloth towel and place the bundle in a reusable plastic bag and refrigerate. Beetroots can be bundled and refrigerated with greens attached.

Favorite and recommended varieties:

- **Touchstone Gold Beetroot:** A reliable golden beet that is delicious and doesn't stain like red beetroot.

- **Chioggia Guardsmark Beetroot:** An Italian heirloom with a stunning white and red interior.

- **Bright Lights Swiss Chard:** Multicolored Swiss chard.

Recipes:

- Beet, Feta, and Herb Salad (Page 154)
- Roasted Beet and Zucchini Salad (Page 158)
- Curried Lentils and Greens (Page 172)
- Refrigerator Pickle, 7 Ways (Page 205)

Asian Greens

[Brassica juncea and Brassica rapa]

Colloquially referred to as Asian greens, these two crop species include a number of cultivars with similar growth habits and requirements, such as giant red mustard, bok choy, komatsuna, mizuna, and tatsoi. These nutrient-dense staples of East Asian cuisine are gaining traction elsewhere because of their flavor and texture. Many commercially available spring salad mixes include baby leaf Asian greens that add bitterness and pepperiness to baby lettuce, which on its own can be quite bland. These fast-growing greens are a must in my spring and fall gardens. After a long brutal winter, it's incredibly rewarding to harvest fresh homegrown greens right from my backyard.

Growth pattern: Since they thrive in cooler temperatures, they are excellent cultivars to grow before the warm-weather crops are ready to be transplanted. Typically, these crops are grown as single plants, although some, such as mustard greens, can be sown densely and harvested when the leaves are still young.

Growing difficulty level: Easy.

Suitability for small spaces and balconies: Suitable. They can either be grown densely in shallow containers and harvested as baby leaf greens or in larger containers and/or in-ground and allowed to mature.

Common issues: Flea beetles, cabbage butterfly, slugs, and damping off (seedling stage).

Tips for success:
- In regions where the spring season is short, get a head start by starting seedlings indoors 4 weeks before you intend to transplant.
- In milder regions, Asian greens can be grown over the winter months.

How to maintain healthy plants:
- Although pest pressure is generally low in the spring, it is still good practice to cover these crops with an insect barrier.
- Weather patterns can be quite unpredictable in the spring. Be prepared to cover these temperature-sensitive crops with frost cover or shade cloth as needed.

When and how to harvest: For larger varieties like giant red mustard and Joi Choi, harvest outer leaves first as needed so the plants can continue to grow and push out new leaves from the center. For smaller varieties like bok choy and tatsoi, harvest whole plants at the soil line. When these crops begin to bolt (flower), harvest the entire plant as the flavor will deteriorate quickly.

Storage tips: If not using your harvest right away, wash, thoroughly spin-dry, and store leaves in a reusable plastic bag in the fridge. Alternatively, you can blanch, squeeze as much water out of the leaves as possible, and freeze for future use.

Favorite and recommended varieties:
- **Joi Choi F1:** Reliable with large dense leaves.
- **Mizuna:** Fast-growing, mild-flavored green that can be eaten raw or cooked.
- **Giant red mustard:** Beautiful purple leaves that can be used in similar ways to kale.

Recipes:
- Charred Bok Choy (Page 190)

Peas

[Pisum sativum]

Peas are a cool-weather staple in home gardens. Loved by children and adults alike, they are versatile, delicious, and nutritious. Not only are the pea pods and seeds edible, but so are the young tender vines and leaves. Peas can be grown for their pods and seeds, or their greens (the young shoots) can be used as microgreens. The flavor and sweetness of freshly picked homegrown peas are unparalleled. They are a great garden snack, and if I'm being completely honest, most don't make it back to my kitchen.

Growth pattern: Peas are vining crops and require trellising. They can also be grown vertically on an A-frame structure or a tomato cage. Seeds should be sown when soil is workable in the spring and nighttime temperatures are no less than 39°F/4°C. They can withstand a light frost and will rebound quickly. Peas prefer to be directly sown; however, in regions where the spring season is short, they may be started indoors for a head start. Refer to the seed packet for timing. After germinating, the vines will grow until they reach a certain height and begin to flower.

Dwarf or bush pea varieties are available. These varieties do not vine as aggressively as standard peas and require minimal to no trellising.

Growing difficulty level: Easy to intermediate. They require minimal maintenance and will grow well as long as their needs are met.

Suitability for small spaces and balconies: Standard vining varieties are not recommended for balconies. Select bush or dwarf varieties for small spaces.

Common issues: Aphids, powdery mildew, damping off (seedling stage), rodents.

Tips for success:

- Soak your peas for 12–24 hours before planting to help speed up the germination process.

- Trellises should be in place at planting time to avoid disruption to the root structure later on.

How to maintain healthy plants: Peas require little to no maintenance at all. Monitor for pest and disease pressure regularly as you would any other crop in your garden. Harvest frequently to encourage the vines to keep producing.

When and how to harvest:

- Shelling peas should be harvested when the pods are full and plump. Snow peas should be harvested when the flat pods just begin to show immature seeds inside. You'll know when that happens because small bumps will begin to appear on the pod. Snap peas should be harvested when the pods begin to plump but before the seeds have a chance to grow.

- When harvesting, carefully pinch or cut the pods from the vine. Tugging to harvest the pods may result in damage to the vines.

Storage tips: Store snap and snow peas in a paper bag in the refrigerator. Shelling peas can be stored whole in the fridge or shelled right away. Shelled peas can be frozen for future use.

Favorite and recommended varieties:

- **Sugar Ann:** Quickly maturing snap pea with a compact growth habit.
- **Strike:** Sweet, early maturing shelling pea.
- **Avalanche:** Productive variety with manageable vines.

Recipes:

- Spring Pesto (Page 163)
- Burrata and Spring Pesto Toast (Page 131)

Onions, Shallots, Leeks, and Scallions

[Allium]

This genus includes a variety of edible crops such as onions, shallots, leeks, and scallions (a.k.a. green or spring onions). While onions and shallots are cultivated for their bulb, leeks are cultivated for their stalk. Spring onions are typically immature onions harvested before bulbing occurs. There are other scallion varietals like Chinese scallion and Welsh onion. Chives are also part of this genus but are typically treated as a perennial herb.

Although temperature, soil health, pest pressure, and watering also influence onion growth, the number of hours of daylight determines when onion plants begin to bulb. When the required number of hours is reached, onions switch focus from leaf growth to bulb formation. Onions are classified into three categories, depending on where you live.

- **Long-Day Onions:** Begin to bulb when day-length is 14–16 hours and grow best above latitude 37° N.
- **Intermediate-Day Onions:** Begin to bulb when day-length is 12–14 hours between latitude 32° N and 42° N.
- **Short-Day Onions:** Begin to bulb when day-length is 10–12 hours and grow best below latitude 35° N.

Growth pattern: Onions and shallots can be grown from set, seed, or seedling. Starting them off either from seed or from seedlings in the spring is favored in regions where spring is short. Sets are immature bulbs that can be planted in early spring (or in certain regions, in fall or winter). They are prone to bolting in regions with short springs, and for that reason I avoid them.

Leeks require special consideration as they are cultivated for their white stalks. If exposed to the sun, a leek stalk will turn green through photosynthesis. Although edible, green leek stalks are not as tender, delicious, or desirable. To maintain white stalks, you will need to blanch your leeks (a process of cutting off the light).

Growing difficulty level: Easy to intermediate. Generally speaking, these are easy crops to grow, but they do require proper curing for long-term storage.

Suitability for small spaces and balconies: It depends. Larger bulbing varieties and leeks are not suitable for container growing. Scallions, on the other hand, can grow well in small spaces and containers. Due to the fact they are low-yield and have special requirements, I generally do not recommend growing bulbing onions and leeks in small gardens.

Common issues: Leek moth, onion maggot, thrips, downy mildew, and damping off (seedling stage).

Tips for success:

- If you have a history of leek moth in your region, consider netting your allium crops to prevent the moths from laying eggs.
- Transplant leek seedlings into a 5" (13cm) deep trench or an underfilled raised bed in preparation for blanching later on in the season.

How to maintain healthy plants:

- Observe foliage regularly for signs of pests or disease.
- Blanch your leeks 3 weeks before you expect to harvest. To accomplish this, backfill the trench or raised bed with soil. Alternatively, you can cut off the light by using cardboard tubes, straw mulch, newspaper, or other DIY contraptions.

When and how to harvest: You'll know onions and shallots are almost ready to harvest when their tops flop over. When this occurs, stop active watering and leave the onions and shallots in the ground for another 1–2 weeks. Harvest by gently pulling on the stems or the bulb itself if you can get a good grip. If needed, use a garden fork to loosen up the soil. Gently remove any large clumps of soil from the roots. Leaving roots and stems intact, lay the onions and shallots on a table or bench in a covered area like a porch, under a gazebo, or in a shed to cure. The ideal curing temperature is 75°F–80°F (24°C–27°C). If you cannot cure the bulbs under these conditions, you can do so in a garage or a warm room in your home.

Leeks are harvested as needed (follow indications for days to maturity, a.k.a. DTM, on the seed packet or from the supplier). The goal is to harvest leeks before they begin to bulb so you end up with a uniform shaft. Scallions can be harvested as needed by trimming off the green parts of the plant. You can also harvest the entire scallion plant once it reaches ½" (1cm) in width.

Storage tips: After curing is complete, trim the roots and stems off your onions and shallots and store your harvest in a cool, dark place like a pantry or basement. Leeks and scallions can be stored in your refrigerator.

Favorite and recommended varieties:

- **Walla Walla Onion:** Very popular mild and sweet variety.
- **Zebrune Shallot:** A French heirloom variety with a delicate flavor.
- **King Richard Leek:** A standard leek variety that matures early.

Recipes:

- Refrigerator Pickle, 7 Ways (Page 205)
- Fermented Hot Sauce (Page 206)
- Harvest Giardiniera (Page 209)

Potatoes

[Solanum tuberosum]

Native to southern Peru and northwestern Bolivia, the potato is now a staple food that is cultivated around the world. From French fries to vodka, potato uses seem to be endless. The flavor of freshly harvested new potatoes is divine.

Growth pattern: What makes potatoes different from other crops is that potato plants do not typically begin their life from seed but from a seed potato. A seed potato is not a seed, but rather an actual potato cultivated for the purpose of sprouting and replanting. I recommend only using certified organic seed potatoes when you grow potatoes in your garden. This helps mitigate a host of problems that can arise from trying to regrow store-bought potatoes that may have been sprayed with an anti-sprouting agent or may have diseases that could spread in your garden.

As the seed potato grows, it produces a main stem with leaves aboveground. Underground, tubers form on lateral stems above the seed potato. Tubers exposed to sunlight may turn green and produce solanine, a toxic compound that can cause digestive issues if consumed. To avoid this, it is recommended to hill your potato vines multiple times a season. You can do this by shoring up the potato plants with more soil and creating mounds in which more tubers can sprout and grow. Hilling should also increase yields.

The same technique can be adapted when growing potatoes in tall bags. When planting out initially, it is recommended to roll the sides of the bag down. This allows the vines to grow with increased access to sunlight. As the potato vines grow, the bag is unrolled in stages and more potting mix is added. The process is repeated until the bag is completely unrolled, upright, and backfilled with potting mix.

Growing difficulty level: Easy. In many ways, growing potatoes is a set-it-and-forget-it activity that requires minimal maintenance.

Suitability for small spaces and balconies: Not suitable. Although it is possible to grow potatoes in a container or grow bag, the yields are simply not worth it if you are working with a small garden or balcony.

Common issues: Colorado potato beetle, scab, early blight, late blight.

Tips for success:

- Select organic, disease-free certified seed potatoes. I advise against sprouting and growing store-bought potatoes.

- Pre-sprouting potatoes (a.k.a. chitting) for 2–3 weeks before planting out will help you determine if your tubers are viable. Simply place potatoes on a tray or in a cardboard egg carton in a cool room in your home.

How to maintain healthy plants:

- Consistently monitor the vines for pest pressure and diseases. Hill vines as needed to increase yields and prevent tubers from turning green.

- If growing potatoes in bags or containers, regular watering will be required.

When and how to harvest:

For new potatoes: You can begin to harvest new potatoes 3–4 weeks after the vines flower. These potatoes will not be suitable for storage and should be eaten right away. Simply dig your hand in and around the vines and carefully pull baby tubers as needed without severely disturbing the plant or root structure.

For the main crop: I prefer to wait until the vines die back completely before I consider harvesting my potatoes. This is the telltale sign that the tubers are now mature. Stop watering and cut the dead vines back.

Let the potatoes sit in the ground or container/grow bag for 10 days so that the skins can toughen up. If heavy rains are expected, cover your containers or beds as excess moisture at this stage may lead to rot.

Carefully dig up your potatoes or invert containers on a tarp. Gently rub off any large chunks of soil and place the tubers in shallow cardboard boxes or trays. Freshly harvested potatoes will need to cure for up to 2 weeks in a cool, dry, and dark space like a basement or well-ventilated shed. The ideal curing temperature is 45ºF–60ºF (7ºC–16ºC).

Storage tips: Store cured potatoes in a cool dark place. Most homes do not have a root cellar, so your basement is the best option as long as excess humidity is not a problem.

Favorite and recommended varieties:

- **French Fingerling:** Delicious, delicate tubers that elevate roast potatoes to the next level.
- **Yukon Gold:** Standard, reliable, and multi-purpose variety.

Recipes:

- Smashed Potatoes with Ají (Page 181)

Spinach

[Spinacia oleracea]

Incredibly cold-hardy, versatile, and nutrient-dense, this leafy green is native to Central and Western Asia. Spinach can be categorized as savoy, semi-savoy, or smooth. Savoy varieties are deeply crinkled and have a higher cold tolerance. They tend to be more difficult to clean. Semi-savoy varieties are less crinkled and have more of an upright growth habit. Smooth varieties, as the name suggests, have smooth spade-shaped leaves with an upright growth habit. One of the earliest greens to mature in the spring garden, I use it in smoothies and salads. Although botanically not spinach, New Zealand and Malabar spinach are good alternatives as they can be consumed in much the same way and are heat tolerant.

Growth pattern: Spinach grows low to the ground, making it difficult to maintain and harvest in traditional beds. It is well suited for raised beds and containers. It is incredibly sensitive to heat and quick to bolt.

Growing difficulty level: Easy.

Suitability for small spaces and balconies: Spinach can certainly be grown in containers and small spaces.

Common issues: Leaf miner, bacterial leaf spot, downy mildew, and damping off (seedling stage).

Tips for success:
- In colder regions, spinach seeds should be sown outdoors as soon as the soil is workable in the spring and the nighttime temperatures are 39°F/4°C or higher.
- In regions with milder winters, spinach can be grown through the cool season.
- If you experience a short spring, consider starting spinach seeds indoors 3–4 weeks before you intend to transplant them to help maximize the harvest in your short cool-weather growing season. Caveat: Spinach seedlings are prone to stress and may bolt prematurely.

How to maintain healthy plants: Because spinach, like Swiss chard and beets, is susceptible to leaf miner damage, it is advisable to cover your crop with an insect barrier or row cover. This prevents the fly from laying eggs on the underside of leaves.

When and how to harvest: You can begin harvesting spinach as needed by plucking or cutting the more mature outer leaves while leaving the center of each plant undisturbed to continue to grow. Harvest until the plants inevitably bolt.

Storage tips: If not using your harvest right away, wash, thoroughly spin-dry, and store leaves in a reusable plastic bag in the fridge. Alternatively, you can blanch, squeeze as much water out of the leaves as possible, and freeze for future use.

Favorite and recommended varieties:
- **Bloomsdale:** Savoyed heirloom variety that can withstand some heat pressure.
- **Space F1:** Fast-growing smooth-leaf variety.

Recipes:
- Risotto with Spring Greens and Asparagus (Page 170)
- Curried Lentils and Greens (Page 172)

Warm-Weather Crops

Tomatoes

[Solanum lycopersicum]

Tomatoes are native to Central America and western South America. They are part of the Solanaceae family, also referred to as Nightshades, and are related to peppers, eggplants, and potatoes. They are believed to have been domesticated by the indigenous peoples of Mexico. Tomatoes traveled east to Europe by way of the Spanish conquistadors, after which they spread throughout the rest of Europe and beyond. A staple of Mediterranean cuisine, it is not surprising that many people do not know that the humble tomato originated thousands of miles away.

Culturally, tomatoes have played a significant part in my upbringing. They show up in many of the recipes my mother prepared growing up. My grandmother and father grew them in our gardens. On a personal note, I think tomatoes are a joy to photograph and create new and exciting recipes with. They are versatile and delicious.

Growth pattern: Tomatoes evolved as vining plants (indeterminate growth pattern), meaning they can grow several feet long and continue to produce off-shoots (also known as suckers), which then in turn start producing flowers and fruit. Determinate varieties (also referred to as bush or patio tomatoes) are bred not to vine uncontrollably like indeterminate types. Dwarf (or micro) tomatoes refer to special varieties bred to remain compact. They are primarily grown indoors, either hydroponically or in soil for year-round harvest. It is important to note that the yield from dwarf tomatoes is not significant and I do not recommend growing them outdoors.

Growing difficulty level: Intermediate. Tomato plants are prone to pest and disease pressure. They require regular pruning and maintenance, making them tricky for the first-time gardener, especially in an urban or suburban setting where space is at a premium. I still highly recommend growing tomatoes as they are essential to a beautiful and abundant garden.

Suitability for small spaces and balconies: I recommend focusing on determinate varieties when growing on a balcony. When searching for seeds or seedlings, look for labels that include words such as determinate, bush, compact, and/or patio.

Common issues: Tomato hornworms, flea beetles, early blight, late blight, Septoria leaf spot.

Tips for success:

- Tomatoes are heavy feeders. Make sure that your garden beds are amended well in the spring.
- Stake or cage your tomato plants early and tie them back regularly so that they are supported. This also reduces the risk of damage from strong winds.
- Grow a variety of colors, shapes, and textures so that you can enjoy everything tomatoes have to offer.

How to maintain healthy plants:

- Keep your plants healthy and thriving by regularly pruning yellow or diseased foliage. Be on the lookout for pests. Continuously tie back or stake your vines as needed.

- Adopt a regular feeding schedule. This is critical for container-grown tomatoes. Organic fertilizers with higher proportions of phosphorous (P) and potassium (K) than nitrogen (N) are suitable.

When and how to harvest: I tend to harvest my tomatoes before they are fully ripe and let them continue to ripen on my kitchen counter. I do this for several reasons. First of all, some pests will seek out ripe or overripe fruit to consume. By harvesting the fruit just before it is fully ripe, I can mitigate the risk of attacks from pests. Secondly, regular harvesting encourages the plant to send out more flowers that will transform into luscious fruit. Deciding on when to harvest under-ripe tomatoes depends on their color (or stage). Tomato colors are categorized as follows:

- Green (still developing, unripe)
- Breaker (when a break or change in the color from green is starting to be evident)
- Turning (when 10–30% of the fruit is red, or whatever the final color of the variety is)
- Pink (when 30–60% of the fruit is red, or whatever the final color of the variety is)
- Light Red (when 60–90% of the fruit is red, or whatever the final color of the variety is)
- Red (when 90+% of the fruit is red, or whatever the final color of the variety is)

When picking underripe tomatoes, it is best to harvest them when they are in the light red stage. If you harvest too early, the fruit may not develop fully and the flavor may not be ideal.

Storage tips: Freshly harvested tomatoes should not be refrigerated. They can be kept on the counter to continue ripening. Do not overcrowd them or place them in closed containers or bags as this will hasten the ripening process and may lead to spoilage too quickly. If you feel the tomatoes are beginning to soften or crack, consider refrigerating them or freezing them to use at a later time.

Favorite and recommended varieties:

Slicers:
- **Black Krim:** Old heirloom variety from Crimea with dark shoulders and juicy interior.
- **Brandywine:** Classic heirloom slicer perfect for sandwiches and tomato toasts.

Cherry/Grape:
- **Juliet:** One of the best grape tomatoes, and perfect for fresh eating and roasting.
- **Blush:** Elongated orange/yellow variety that is well suited to salads.
- **Blue Berry:** Small, round variety packed full of anthocyanin.

Paste (sauce):
- **San Marzano:** Classic Italian heirloom with a compact growth habit.

Recipes:
- Summer Tomato Toast (Page 132)
- Tomato Tart (Page 136)
- Hummus with Blistered Cherry Tomatoes (Page 139)
- Maha's Chopped Salad (Page 153)
- Peach Panzanella-Style Salad (Page 157)
- Roasted Tomato Sauce (Page 167)
- Pasta alla Norma (Page 177)

Peppers

[Capsicum]

Native to the Americas, this heat-loving member of the nightshade family is now cultivated worldwide for its flavor, versatility, and culinary uses. *Capsicum* traveled east to Europe by way of the Spanish conquistadors in the same way many other crops did. When Europeans encountered *capsicum* fruits, they called them peppers, because like black pepper (of the genus *Piper*, native to India), they can be spicy.

Whether you call them capsicums, peppers, chilis, or chiles, these fruits trace back to the genus *Capsicum*. Within this genus, there are five domesticated and cultivated species:

- *Capsicum annuum* is the most widely cultivated and includes varieties like bell peppers, jalapeños, cayenne, and New Mexico chiles, to name a few.

- *Capsicum chinense* includes culinary staples like habanero and Scotch bonnets.

- *Capsicum frutescens* includes unique varieties like the tabasco pepper, the peri-peri, and Wiri Wiri from Guyana.

- *Capsicum pubescens* is a less common cultivar and genetically distinct, with its hairy leaves and black-colored seeds. The most well-known variety in this cultivar is the rocoto.

- *Capsicum baccatum* is a personal favorite and includes varieties like the ají amarillo and ají limón.

Some like it hot, and I certainly do. Peppers are incredibly versatile. They can be grilled, roasted, stuffed, fried, pickled, fermented, dried, or turned into sauces, condiments, and so much more.

Growth pattern: Pepper plants are for the most part compact and sturdy. Some varieties will grow tall and lanky, while others will remain short and bushy. They require staking or caging to keep them from toppling over under the weight of the fruit. My preference is to use bamboo stakes and regularly tie the plants back so they remain stable all season long. It may not look like it at first, but once your plants begin to fruit, they will become quite top-heavy. Their main stem will remain relatively small. Therefore, supporting them will be critical to achieving success and abundance.

Growing difficulty level: Easy to intermediate. Although they are prone to some disease and pest pressure like other nightshades, pepper plants tend to perform well as long as their needs are met.

Suitability for small spaces and balconies: Peppers are a perfect crop to grow on balconies and in small spaces. They thrive in containers because they do not have to compete with other crops for nutrients. Make sure to select a suitable container and maintain your plants regularly. I recommend focusing on small-fruited varieties when growing in small spaces. Larger fruited varieties (such as bell peppers) do not produce many fruits per plant. Smaller fruited varieties tend to outperform their large-fruited siblings.

Common issues: Powdery mildew, bacterial leaf spot, flea beetles, aphids, pepper maggots.

How to maintain healthy plants:

- Adopt a regular feeding schedule. This is critical for container-grown peppers. Organic fertilizers with higher proportions of phosphorous (P) and potassium (K) than nitrogen (N) are recommended.

- Just like with any other crop, vigilance and observation are key. Keep a lookout for pests and diseases. Regularly remove and discard yellowing leaves.

When and how to harvest:

- Some peppers are best harvested before they are fully ripe. For example, jalapeño peppers are harvested when they are still green. If you leave them on the plant too long, they will mature and turn red (but if they do, they are certainly still usable and delicious). Aleppo or bull's horn peppers are harvested when fully ripe and bright red. If you pick your peppers prematurely, there is no guarantee they will ripen on the counter. The flavor of an underripe pepper will differ from that of a ripe pepper. If you're not sure at which stage to harvest a specific variety, consult the seed packet. The seed packet will typically show a photo of the fruit at the right harvesting stage.

- Picking fruit regularly encourages the plant to send out more flowers, which will eventually turn to fruit. Don't let your ripe peppers sit on the vine too long. They could begin to dry out or even rot. Some peppers can easily be hand-picked off the vines, while others may require pruners or kitchen scissors. Avoid tugging on

Tips for success:

- Grow varieties suited for your climate and zone. If your warm season is short, consider growing small-fruited, quick-to-mature varieties.

- Pepper plants are heavy feeders. Ensure your beds and containers are amended and prepared adequately in the spring.

- Pepper plants don't need to be constantly watered. They do well when the soil dries up slightly between watering sessions. They don't like to grow in a soggy medium, so a little neglect might help them thrive.

your plants unnecessarily or you may end up with an entire branch in your hands.

Storage tips: Store your peppers in trays, paper bags, or open vessels. You do not need to refrigerate them right away. I recommend not refrigerating them unless you have processed them. If they begin to soften, you can then refrigerate them to buy a couple of additional days. Freezing hot peppers whole in freezer bags is also an option. You can then use what you need in salsas, sauces, chutneys, chilis, and curries all year round. Note that a pepper's heat level tends to decrease after being frozen, so you may need to adjust quantities.

Favorite and recommended varieties:

- **Jimmy Nardello:** A mild Italian heirloom, it produces long red fruits that can be eaten fresh or cooked.

- **Bull's horn:** This mild variety also goes by Corno di Toro. Available in yellow and red, this variety is versatile and has many uses.

- **Serrano:** Hot Mexican variety that can be used across multiple cuisines and in various preparations. More versatile than jalapeños, in my opinion.

- **Aleppo:** A Syrian heirloom with a storied history; they are typically dried and turned into flakes.

Recipes:

- Garden-Inspired Libations (Page 119)
- Roasted Tomatillo Salsa Verde (Page 144)
- Maha's Chopped Salad (Page 153)
- Hand-Chopped Chimichurri (Page 194)
- Salsa Macha (Page 195)
- Ají (Page 196)
- Shattah (Page 197)
- Refrigerator Pickles, 7 Ways (Page 205)
- Fermented Hot Sauce (Page 206)
- Harvest Giardiniera (Page 209)

Eggplants

[Solanum melongena]

Whether you call these fruits eggplants, aubergines, or brinjals, one thing is for certain: they are cultivated worldwide and are considered staples in Middle Eastern, Mediterranean, East Asian, South Asian, and Southeast Asian cuisines, among others. They are nightshades and thrive in warm climates just like their tomato and pepper relatives. Eggplants are culturally significant for me and were on the dinner table regularly while I was growing up. As an adult, I have grown to appreciate them grilled, roasted, stuffed, pureed, stir-fried, and stewed. They have a meaty texture and can be a great meat substitute in many recipes and preparations.

Growth pattern: Sturdy plants that require staking or caging to avoid damage from strong winds or the weight of their fruits. I do not prune any branches and allow the plants to do their thing all season long.

Growing difficulty level: Easy to intermediate. Although they are prone to some disease and pest pressure like other nightshades, eggplants tend to perform well as long as they are well maintained.

Suitability for small spaces and balconies: Eggplants are an ideal crop to grow on balconies and in small spaces. They thrive in containers and grow bags, especially when they don't have to compete with other crops. I recommend focusing on small-fruited varieties (for example, Gretel or fairy tale) as they will be more abundant. Larger fruited varieties (for example, black beauty) do not produce many fruits per plant.

Common issues: Japanese beetles, flea beetles, spider mites, blight.

Tips for success:

- Grow varieties suited for your climate and zone. If your warm season is short, select small-fruited varieties with shorter DTM (days to maturity).

- Eggplants are heavy feeders. Ensure your beds and containers are amended and prepared adequately in the spring. Select containers with a capacity of at least 7 gallons (27L) per plant.

How to maintain healthy plants:

- Adopt a regular feeding schedule. This is especially critical for container-grown eggplants. Organic fertilizers with higher proportions of phosphorous (P) and potassium (K) than nitrogen (N) are suitable.

- Keep a lookout for pests and diseases. Regularly remove and discard yellowing leaves to mitigate disease and increase airflow.

When and how to harvest: Eggplants are consumed before they are ripe. If allowed to ripen, the fruit will turn yellow, the seed cavity will swell, and the fruit will become unappetizing. With so many varieties available, check your seed packet or supplier website for pictures that demonstrate the ideal harvest size. I tend to harvest eggplants on the smaller side as I prefer them meatier and with little to no seeds.

Storage tips: I recommend harvesting eggplants as needed to avoid spoilage. Store freshly harvested eggplants on your counter, in an open bowl or tray. Use them as soon as possible. If they begin to soften, refrigerate them to increase their shelf life by a few more days. For long-term storage, you can roast them and freeze the pulp.

Favorite and recommended varieties:

- **Ping Tung Long Eggplant:** An Asian variety well suited for frying.
- **Rosa Bianca:** Italian heirloom with beautiful coloration. Ideal for roasting and pureeing.
- **Fairy Tale F1:** Prolific small-fruited variety.

Recipes:

- Mutabal (Page 140)
- Roasted Beet and Zucchini Salad (Page 158)
- Stuffed Eggplant (Page 174)
- Pasta alla Norma (Page 177)
- Grilled Eggplant with Garlic Yogurt (Page 185)

Beans

[Phaseolus vulgaris]

Native to the Americas, common beans have been in cultivation for thousands of years. They are historically significant and a major component of diets around the world.

Beans are also nitrogen fixers, meaning that they can fix, or supply, nitrogen to the soil by a process called biological nitrogen fixation. This process is prevalent in other members of the *Fabaceae* family, which includes other *Phaseolus* species. Bean plants contain symbiotic rhizobia bacteria within nodules in their root systems. These nodules produce nitrogen compounds that help the plant grow. When the plant dies, the fixed nitrogen is released into the soil. For this reason, it is considered good practice to leave legume roots in the soil after harvest.

Beans are an integral part of the Three Sisters Indigenous planting technique, along with maize (corn) and squash. Beans are planted around the base of corn stalks and allowed to twist and vine upwards. In a way, corn acts as a trellis or stake for the beans to climb. Squash is planted in the space between patches of corn and beans. The corn and beans provide the squash cover from the blazing sun, while the squash shades the soil to reduce water evaporation. The spiky nature of squash vines makes it uncomfortable for pests such as rats and raccoons to reach the corn.

Freshly picked beans are crisp and sweet. The ability to walk into the garden and harvest a handful of green (or purple or yellow) beans at their peak is one of summer's greatest pleasures.

Growth pattern: Beans can be classified as bush (dwarf) or pole (climbing). Bush beans have a compact growth habit that makes them ideal for small space gardening and container gardening. They generally don't grow taller than 2' (60cm). Pole beans, on the other hand, are traditional climbers that require trellising or staking and can grow upwards of 10' (3m). Beans are considered a warm-weather crop.

Growing difficulty level: Easy. Beans prefer to be directly sown, meaning that they don't require any indoor seed starting equipment or lights. As long as the seeds germinate and they have a structure to climb (pole beans), they will generally perform well and provide you with an abundant harvest.

Suitability for small spaces and balconies: For small spaces, I recommend focusing on bush bean varieties.

Common issues: Japanese beetles, spider mites, bean leaf beetle, cutworms, bacterial leaf disease.

Tips for success:

- If growing pole beans, ensure you have a solid trellis or support structure in place at planting time. Structures should be at least 8' (2.5 m) tall.

- Direct sowing is ideal as beans don't appreciate being transplanted. Seeds can be soaked in water for 12–24 hours before planting to help speed up germination.

How to maintain healthy plants: Beans require little to no maintenance at all. Monitor for pest and disease pressure regularly as you would any other crop in your garden. Harvest often to encourage the vines to keep producing.

When and how to harvest:

- For fresh/green beans: Beans should be harvested when they are still immature (when they reach the length and thickness you desire and before the seeds inside the pod swell to the point of being visible).

- For dry beans: Allow the bean pods to fully mature and dry on the vine. Harvest when the bean pods are yellow and completely dehydrated.

Storage tips:

- For fresh/green beans: I recommend you only harvest what you need for a given recipe or meal. However, if you must harvest a large quantity for storage, place green beans in a reusable plastic bag or container and refrigerate until needed. Alternatively, you can blanch the beans in boiling water for 30 seconds, shock them in ice water, bag them, and freeze them for future use.

- For dry beans: Once beans are fully dried, shell them and store them in an airtight container like a mason jar. Alternatively, you can freeze the beans to help prevent a possible bean weevil outbreak.

Favorite and recommended varieties:

- **Romano Bean:** Classic Italian heirloom with flat pods.

- **Dragon Tongue:** Dutch heirloom with striking yellow and purple streaks. Can be consumed as a fresh bean or allowed to mature and saved for use as a dry bean.

- **Maxibel:** A French filet bean, delicate and thin.

Recipes:

- Green Beans with Coriander and Garlic (Page 182)
- Refrigerator Pickle, 7 Ways (Page 205)

Cucumbers

[Cucumis sativus]

What would summer be without crunchy, juicy cucumbers? Native to South Asia, cucumbers are now widely cultivated around the world. They are in the cucurbit plant family, along with squash, pumpkin, zucchini, bitter melon, watermelon, cantaloupe, and gourds. Varieties are typically classified as pickling, slicing, or greenhouse. Pickling cucumbers, as the name suggests, are varieties intended for pickling or fermenting. They are shorter, bulkier, and have thicker skin, so they tend to remain crispy and firm after the pickling process. Slicing varieties are typically longer and thinner than pickling varieties and are intended to be consumed fresh. Greenhouse varieties are bred to be more suitable for greenhouse-growing conditions. Some are parthenocarpic, meaning that they do not need pollination to set fruit, making them ideal for greenhouse production. Parthenocarpic varieties produce almost seedless fruit and can also be grown in a home garden.

Some of my earliest childhood food memories include cucumbers. They were always on the dining table, next to some labneh and za'atar. I'm also a serial preserver and love nothing more than pickling homegrown summer cucumbers to enjoy in the middle of winter.

Growth pattern: Cucumbers are vining crops much like their cucurbit relative, squash. Although they can happily grow on the ground and vine as they please, it is preferable to train them up a trellis or some other form of support to keep the fruit off the ground. With trellising, the fruit grows straighter and is protected from ground-level pest pressure.

There are also bush or patio varieties on the market that have been bred for compact growth.

Growing difficulty level: Easy to intermediate. Cucumbers not only require supporting and/or trellising, they also must be regularly inspected for pests and disease.

Suitability for small spaces and balconies: Patio or bush varieties will work well on balconies and in small spaces. Standard varieties will also work in small spaces as long as the vines are managed.

Common issues: Cucumber beetles, bacterial wilt, powdery mildew.

Tips for success:

- Although you can start cucumbers indoors or in a greenhouse, they are prone to transplant shock and prefer to be directly sown.

- As heat lovers, they should only be planted out when daytime temperatures are 65°F–75°F (18°C–23°C) and nighttime temperatures do not go below 50°F (10°C).

- Vining varieties will require trellising and support. Ensure that your supports are in place at planting time.

How to maintain healthy plants:

- Remove or prune away diseased or dying foliage to reduce the chance of spread and to increase airflow.

- If you live in an area where cucumber beetles are prevalent, take the necessary steps to deal with them as they can also be a vector for bacterial wilt.

- Consider fertilizing throughout the growing season with an organic fertilizer with higher proportions of phosphorous (P) and potassium (K) than nitrogen (N) to encourage flowering and fruit production.

When and how to harvest:
- Cucumbers are consumed before they are ripe. If allowed to ripen, the fruit will turn yellow and unappetizing. With so many varieties available, check your seed packet or supplier website for harvesting information and pictures to get a feel for what the fruit should look like when ready for harvest.

- There is no harm in harvesting a cucumber prematurely. The lovable gherkin pickle is an immature cucumber harvested early.

Storage tips: Refrigerate after harvest.

Favorite and recommended varieties:
- **Suyo Long:** A long-fruited variety from China, these are great in salads and can also be quick-pickled.

- **Marketmore 76:** Old faithful! An open-pollinated tried-and-true variety.

- **Itachi F1:** A very unique Asian type of cucumber with white skin, this variety adds visual interest to salads and other preparations.

Recipes:
- Cucumber Yogurt Dip (Page 143)
- Maha's Chopped Salad (Page 153)
- Refrigerator Pickle, 7 Ways (Page 205)

Zucchini and Squash

[Cucurbita pepo]

Fun fact: August 18th is "National Sneak Some Zucchini Onto Your Neighbor's Porch Day." These obscenely prolific crops are members of the cucurbit family and are available in a wide range of colors, shapes, flavors, and textures. Squash can be categorized loosely into two categories. Summer squash (which also includes zucchini and marrow) is cultivated for fresh consumption during the summer months as the name suggests. Summer squash fruit matures quickly and can be eaten right away (cooked or raw). Winter squash varieties are those that mature toward the end of the growing season and may require a curing and storage period, meaning that they would be cooked and consumed in late fall and winter. Squash blossoms are also edible and considered a delicacy. They are typically stuffed, dipped in batter, and fried—a summertime classic.

Growth pattern: Most summer squash varieties grow on compact bushes, while most winter squash grow on long rambling vines. Winter squash can be trained to grow vertically on an arch or trellis.

Growing difficulty level: Easy to intermediate. Zucchini and squash require regular inspection for pests and diseases.

Suitability for small spaces and balconies: Generally speaking, squash and zucchini plants are space hogs, and they are therefore not suitable for small spaces or balconies. They do not perform optimally in containers, so I do not recommend growing them if you have limited space.

Common issues: Cucumber beetles, squash bugs, bacterial wilt, squash vine borer, powdery mildew.

Tips for success:

- For vining varieties, make sure you have ample space for the vines to sprawl. Alternatively, consider growing vining squash crops up a trellis or archway. Not only is this beneficial from a pest pressure and airflow perspective, but it can also be quite architecturally and aesthetically pleasing.

- Although you can start zucchini and squash seeds indoors or in a greenhouse, they are prone to transplant shock and prefer to be directly sown.

- Plant outside when daytime temperatures range 65°F–75°F (18°C–23°C) and nighttime temperatures do not go below 50°F (10°C).

- You may need to manually pollinate these crops, especially if you live in an area with minimal pollinator activity. Hand pollinating squash and zucchini involves manually transferring pollen from the male flower (anther) and applying it to the female flower (stigma) with a paintbrush or via other means. You can tell the flowers apart by their shape. The male flower will be attached to a long skinny stem, whereas the female flower will be attached to the ovary, a small fruit at the base of the flower. Once pollinated, this ovary will swell and grow.

How to maintain healthy plants:

- Remove or prune away diseased or dying foliage to reduce the chance of spread and to increase airflow.

- If you live in an area where cucumber beetles and squash bugs are prevalent, take the necessary steps to manage them as they can also be vectors for disease.

- Consider fertilizing throughout the growing season with an organic fertilizer with a higher proportion of phosphorous (P) and potassium (K) than nitrogen (N) to encourage flowering and fruit production.

When and how to harvest:

- Zucchini and other summer squash varieties can be harvested at any stage before they reach full ripeness. If you allow them to ripen fully, they will not be appealing and will contain a significant number of seeds. They should be harvested while still immature, at maximum flavor and with the smallest seed cavity possible.

- Winter squash varieties are trickier. Each variety will have its telltale sign, and I recommend referring to the information available on the seed packet or from the seed supplier. Generally speaking, you want to wait until the fruit develops a hard rind and

changes to the final (mature) color. After cutting the fruits from the vine, they will need to be cured for 7 days to further harden the skin and prevent spoilage. You can cure them on a table outdoors under the sun or move them indoors and cure them in the warmest room in your house. Some varieties can be consumed right after curing, while others will benefit from long-term storage to fully develop their optimal flavor.

Storage tips: For zucchini and other summer squash, refrigerate after harvest. For winter squash varieties, store them in a cool part of your house such as a basement or cold room (ideally around 55°F/13°C).

Favorite and recommended varieties:

- **Dunja F1:** An early standard dark green zucchini with powdery mildew resistance.

- **Costata Romanesco:** A gray-green ribbed Italian heirloom zucchini, this variety is incredibly prolific and delicious.

- **Robin's Koginut Squash F1:** A winter squash variety bred for flavor and shelf life.

Recipes:

- Autumn Squash toast (Page 135)
- Stuffed Squash Blossoms (Page 147)
- Roasted Beet and Zucchini Salad (Page 158)

Tomatillos and Ground Cherries

[Physalis]

This genus includes a range of crops such as tomatillos (*P. philadelphica*), cape gooseberry (*P. peruviana*), and groundcherry (*P. pruinosa*). There are other species in this genus, however, these are the most commonly grown in the home garden. *Physalis* are warm-weather crops in the nightshade family native to the Americas. What makes these crops so unique is that the fruit is surrounded by an inedible but protective paper-like husk. After pollination, the calyx of the flower surrounds the developing fruit and grows with it, forming the husk. I love homemade salsa verde or green hot sauce, especially when the tomatillos are homegrown, organic, and harvested at their peak.

Growth pattern: Tomatillos can vine uncontrollably, and branches may snap under the weight of the fruit. Supporting them with stakes and/or cages is critical to avoid plant damage and to keep sprawl to a minimum. Like other nightshades, tomatillos and ground cherries will root from the stem. Transplant seedlings deeply by burying part of the stem, as this will cause the plants to sprout new roots.

Growing difficulty level: Easy to intermediate. Generally, these crops are fuss-free and don't require significant maintenance. They adapt well to temperature fluctuations and drought.

Suitability for small spaces and balconies: Not suitable. Although tomatillos and ground cherries will grow in containers, the yields will be low.

Common issues: Three-lined potato beetle, aphids, mosaic virus.

Tips for success:

- Tomatillos are not self-fertile. Grow at least 2 plants to ensure good pollination.

- Tomatillos will require staking and/or caging. Ensure that your supports are in place at planting time.

- Ground cherries will grow closer to the ground but will still benefit from caging to keep as much of the foliage off the ground as possible.

How to maintain healthy plants:

- Regularly tie back and support the vines as they grow. Be on the lookout for pest pressure. Three-lined potato beetles are particularly destructive.

- Tomatillos and ground cherries are both tolerant of poor soil. You may consider fertilizing the soil throughout the season with organic fertilizers containing higher proportions of phosphorous (P) and potassium (K) than nitrogen (N).

When and how to harvest: Tomatillos are harvested before they are fully ripe, as the sour flavor is desirable. They can be harvested when the fruit is still firm and green, and when it fills (or outgrows) the husk.

Ground cherries, on the other hand, should not be actively harvested off the vine. As the name suggests, they are ready to harvest when they fall from the vine. Underripe ground cherries are sour and contain toxic compounds and can cause indigestion and nausea. It is important to consume ground cherries only when they are ripe.

Storage tips: Store tomatillos and ground cherries in paper bags or in an open container or tray on your counter. They will last several days this way. Tomatillos can be husked and frozen whole to be used at a later date.

Favorite and recommended varieties:

- **Toma Verde:** Standard green heirloom tomatillo variety.
- **Aunt Molly's Ground Cherry:** Deliciously sweet fruit on vigorous vines.

Recipes:

- Roasted Tomatillo Salsa Verde (Page 144)

Herbs

This crop guide groups various plant species loosely into the category of herbs because they often have similar requirements. No garden is complete without herbs. They add flavor and color to a variety of dishes, can be used in sweet and savory preparations, and can even be steeped for a warm and comforting herbal tea.

Growth pattern: Different herbs have their specific growth habits, but in general, there is one thing that unites them all. At some point in the growing season, they will flower and potentially go to seed. For some herbs, this is desirable. Dill seed and dill flower heads give that distinct dill pickle flavor. Cilantro seeds can be replanted or dried and ground into coriander spice. Lavender flowers can be used in teas, desserts, or cosmetic applications. Chive flowers are delicious and can be used in vinegar infusions.

For other herbs like Genovese basil, flowering is not desirable and any flower buds should be pruned to encourage the plants to bush out and grow more leaves.

Growing difficulty level: Easy. For woody herbs like rosemary, sage, thyme, and oregano, consider purchasing seedlings from your local nursery or garden center as they are more difficult and time-consuming to start from seed. Herbs such as cilantro, basil, dill, and parsley can be started from seed with minimal effort.

Suitability for small spaces and balconies: Very suitable. Both perennial and annual herbs perform splendidly well in containers and small spaces. If protected well over the cooler months, perennial herbs in containers will come back year after year. Refer to Chapter 10 for potted perennial herb winterization tips.

Common issues: Aphids, caterpillars, powdery mildew, downy mildew.

Tips for success:

- Space out perennial herbs when transplanting them to permanent locations. This gives them a chance to spread and grow into the negative space, resulting in much sturdier and healthier plants that don't have to compete for nutrients.

- Container-grown herbs should be watered regularly since they tend to dry out quickly, causing undue stress on the plants.

How to maintain healthy plants: Regular harvesting encourages the plants to keep producing.

When and how to harvest: Herbs can be harvested as needed by simply cutting the desired quantity. A good rule of thumb is to only harvest up to 1/3 of the plant at a time. This ensures there's enough of the plant left to continue growing without being stressed.

Timing will depend on a few factors such as which part of the plant you are harvesting and how it will be used. Herbs used for foliage such as basil, thyme, rosemary, chervil, and others should be harvested before the plants begin to flower. Regular harvesting allows you to delay the flowering process and keep the plants producing.

Leafy herbs should be harvested by pinching off stems right above a set of leaves (a leaf node). This encourages the plants to sprout new branches, resulting in a bushier plant. Woody herbs such as thyme, rosemary, sage, and oregano can be harvested by cutting sprigs right above a set of leaves 4" (10cm) from the base of the plant. Parsley and cilantro can be harvested by cutting the outer stems at the base of the plant without disturbing the center of the plant where new leaves emerge.

Herbs grown for flowers like lavender and chamomile will have differing requirements and techniques. Calendula and chamomile flowers should be harvested as soon as the petals open. Lavender is ready to harvest when the flowers emerge but right before they open. Lavender is harvested by pruning or cutting right above the first set of leaves on the flower spike. Depending on the variety and maturity of your lavender, the spikes may be long or short.

Herbs grown for their seed, such as dill and coriander spice (cilantro seed), can be harvested after the plants bolt, flower, and set seeds. Wait until the seeds dry completely and change color from green to brown/black before harvesting.

Storage tips: I recommend harvesting only as needed for utmost freshness and flavor. However, if you wish to harvest in large quantities, storage will depend on final use.

Tender herbs like basil, cilantro, parsley, and dill can be stored upright in a mason jar filled ⅓ of the way with water. The mason jar and herbs can stay on the counter for a few hours this way. The jar can be stored directly in the fridge, covered with a loose-fitting reusable plastic bag right over the herbs. Change the water every 2 days. Herbs will stay fresh this way for 7–10 days.

Woody herbs like rosemary, thyme, and sage can be wrapped in a dry paper towel and stored in a reusable plastic bag in the crisper. They will remain fresh for 7–10 days.

Refer to the herb drying primer in Chapter 3.

Favorite and recommended varieties:

If I had to choose 7 must grow herbs, they would be:

Genovese Basil: Excellent all-around variety suitable for pesto, salads, and more.
Santo Cilantro: Reliable slow-bolting variety.

Za'atar: Botanically a variety of oregano, but it can be treated like thyme. Either way, it is versatile and delicious.
Common sage: A must in every home kitchen garden.

Rosemary: Classic herb that is easy to grow.
Giant of Italy Parsley: A high-yield flat-leaf variety.
Teddy Dill: Productive variety that is slow to bolt offering up delicious fronds and aromatic seed heads.

Recipes:

Garden-Inspired Libations (Page 119)
Roasted Tomatillo Salsa Verde (Page 144)

Spring Pesto (Page 163)
Summer Pesto (Page 164)
Hand-Chopped Chimichurri (Page 194)

Ají (Page 196)
Herb Blends (Page 217)
Herb-Infused Salt (Page 219)
Compound Butter (Page 223)

Garlic

[Allium sativum]

Native to central Asia and northeastern Iran, garlic is now used worldwide for culinary, medicinal, and even religious applications. It is in the same plant family as onions and is incredibly easy to grow in the home garden. One of the challenges I have is sourcing good-quality garlic at the grocery store. Most of what's available has been transported thousands of miles and grown in conditions that are dubious at best. Locally grown or homegrown garlic is far superior to store-bought on so many levels—I guarantee that you will taste the difference.

Growth pattern: Garlic varieties are classified as either hardneck or softneck. The neck refers to the stalk that grows up from the garlic clove in the spring. Hardneck garlic produces a stem that becomes rigid as the plant grows and then eventually dries and cures. Softneck garlic produces a soft stalk made up mostly of leaves (no central stalk). The leaves maintain their flexibility as they dry. Hardneck garlic is better suited for colder climates, while softneck garlic is better suited for milder climates.

Although it is certainly possible to grow garlic using store-bought bulbs, selecting good quality, organic, certified disease-free "seed garlic" is preferable. Seed garlic is garlic that is specifically grown and selected for replanting. Since garlic is planted in the fall and harvested in early summer, the timing of your planting will depend on when you expect your first frost (if you get frost).

Growing difficulty level: Easy.

Suitability for small spaces and balconies: Not suitable for containers. If you have a small garden with in-ground or raised beds, you can certainly grow a small patch of garlic.

Common issues: Garlic rust, bulb mites, leek moth.

Tips for success:

- Select good quality, disease-free seed garlic. Separate your seed garlic bulbs into cloves carefully, making sure the papery layers are intact. Prioritize planting the biggest cloves since those will yield bigger bulbs the following year.

- Amend the bed with lots of compost or composted manure, then plant your garlic cloves with the pointy side up 3" (8cm) deep. Water in, mulch, and forget about it until spring.

How to maintain healthy plants:

- Assuming that your cloves were viable and you followed the planting directions properly, you will soon start to see green leaves pushing through the ground. The shoots will grow vigorously through the spring and early summer.

- Although not necessary, you can fertilize with an all-purpose organic fertilizer once in late spring.

- In early summer, hardneck varieties of garlic send up a scape (a round stalk with the garlic flower attached to the tip). The scape will grow upwards and then begin to curl. Once the scape has curled and formed a circle, you should harvest it. You can snap it off with your fingers or a pair of scissors. Avoid accidentally cutting off any leaves in the process. Removing the scape forces the garlic plant to refocus energy on bulb growth, which is exactly what we want: big, aromatic, and healthy garlic bulbs. Scapes are edible and can be eaten raw or cooked.

- Regularly inspect the garlic plants for pests and disease.

When and how to harvest: Discerning when to harvest the bulbs can be tricky, especially for a first-time grower. If you harvest too early, the bulbs will be small and won't store well. If you wait too long, the bulbs may split and lose their protective wrapper. Garlic greens begin to brown and die from the bottom up. Once the bottom 3–4 leaves have died back completely and you have only a few green leaves remaining at the top, carefully dig up one bulb and check the size. If it feels undersized, allow the garlic to continue growing for another 2 weeks.

When ready to harvest, use your hands to remove the soil around the garlic greens, exposing the bulbs below. Carefully pull them up. You can also use a garden fork to loosen the soil. However, if this is your first year growing garlic, err on the side of caution and use your hands. After harvest, carefully remove most of the large clumps of soil from the bulbs without damaging the protective layers. Do not wash your garlic and do not trim the stems or roots.

Curing garlic bulbs is required to guarantee viability for long-term storage. You can hang bundles of 5 or 6 together or lay all your garlic flat on a mesh or screen to ensure good airflow. The best place to do this is a covered porch, shed, or barn away from the sun but with good airflow. You can also cure the garlic in a dry basement. After 2 weeks, the stems and leaves should be completely brown. If you feel they are not quite dry, you can continue to cure them for an additional week.

Storage tips: After curing is complete, trim the roots and stems. Leave behind an inch (2cm) of stem. This helps keep the garlic bulbs intact during storage. Store your garlic in a cool, dark place like a pantry or basement.

Favorite and recommended varieties:

- **Music:** Reliable hardneck variety with large bulbs.
- **Chesnok Red:** Beautiful red-skinned hardneck variety.

Recipes:

- Garlic Confit (Page 213)
- Compound Butter (Page 223)

Chapter 3

Garden-to-Table Recipes & Preservation Techniques

First we grow, then we eat. Well, not quite. The life of a gardener is not about instant gratification. It's about the promise of abundance and sustenance that a single seed can bring. It is about the hard work, with care and appreciation for nature and all she has to offer. Setting the right intentions before the growing season even begins helps guide us all the way to the harvest.

My goal is to share recipes that pair homegrown and seasonal produce with pantry staples. I have included primers on drying, fermenting, pickling, and freezing your harvests, and corresponding recipes to help you enjoy the growing season's bounty well into the winter months. But not everything here is homegrown. It doesn't have to be. No matter where you live, there's probably a farm stand or farmers' market. Support local farmers when you can. Get to know them personally. Ask questions. Buy their produce.

These recipes represent my upbringing and Middle Eastern roots, my love affair with Mediterranean cuisine, and my obsession with South American chiles. These dishes are meant to be shared and enjoyed with friends and loved ones.

I hope this chapter will inspire you to grow some of what you love to eat and think of new flavor and texture combinations. As the American poet Wendell Berry once said, "Eating is an agricultural act." The acts of growing and eating are interconnected and mutually dependent. You cannot have one without the other. As such, these recipes are adaptable. I encourage you to put your own spin on them. Enjoy them and make them your own. If a recipe includes a corresponding QR code, view the digital content as it will showcase a special technique or a similar recipe you might enjoy.

My cooking mantra has always been to taste as I go and make necessary adjustments. That's why for most of the recipes, you'll see that there are no specific quantities for salt and pepper. My advice is to trust your palate. Some recipes, however, include specific salt amounts and should not be modified.

Garden-Inspired Libations

Cheers to a successful and abundant garden. I love to use some of my homegrown herbs, flowers, and produce in different and fun ways. Though these recipes do include alcohol, you can easily substitute an alcohol-free product for the liquor. The mocktail market is expanding at lightning speed, and there are new alcohol-free "liquors" hitting shelves regularly.

Thai Basil Smash

5 Thai basil leaves

2 oz (60ml) dry gin

1 oz (30ml) lemon juice

½ oz (15ml) simple syrup

Basil leaves and lemon twist for garnish

Instructions

In a cocktail shaker, muddle basil leaves. Add gin, lemon juice, and simple syrup. Fill with ice, shake vigorously, and strain into an ice-filled old-fashioned glass. Garnish with basil leaves and lemon twist.

Bourbon Thyme

2 oz (60ml) thyme-
infused bourbon*

¾ oz (20ml) lemon juice

½ oz (15ml) maple syrup

Thyme sprigs and lemon
twist for garnish

Instructions

In a cocktail shaker, add thyme-infused bourbon, lemon juice, and maple syrup. Fill with ice, shake vigorously, and strain into an ice-filled old-fashioned glass (or serve it up in a martini glass or coupe). Garnish with thyme sprigs and lemon twist.

* Thyme-infused bourbon can be prepared by steeping 10 thyme sprigs in a small bottle with bourbon. Don't use fancy bourbon for this recipe. Use a bottle with a tight-fitting lid, and allow the bourbon to steep for at least 3 weeks in a cool dark place like a cupboard.

Paloma Picante

2 oz (60ml) tequila or mezcal (I prefer mezcal)

2 oz (60ml) fresh grapefruit juice

1 oz (30ml) fresh lime juice

½ oz (15ml) chile-infused simple syrup *

Sparkling water (optional)

Tajin chile-lime seasoning to rim the glass

Grapefruit wedge, herbs, and flowers for garnish

Instructions

Using a lime wedge, wet the rim of a tall glass and coat in Tajin chile-lime seasoning. Fill glass with ice and set aside. In a cocktail shaker, add tequila or mezcal, grapefruit juice, lime juice, and chile-infused simple syrup. Fill shaker with ice, shake vigorously, and strain into prepared glass. You can top the drink with sparkling water if you wish. Garnish with grapefruit wedge, herbs, and flowers.

* Chile-infused simple syrup: In a saucepan, combine ½ cup of water, ½ cup of white sugar, and a few dry hot peppers. You can also use fresh sliced jalapeños if you wish. Bring to a boil, turn off the heat, and allow the simple syrup to steep and cool. Strain and store in the fridge. Infused simple syrup will keep for up to a week refrigerated.

Strawberry Rhubarb Shrub (Sipping Vinegar)

Sipping vinegars have been around for hundreds of years. In fifteenth-century England, they were even used to treat ailments like scurvy. In modern times, shrubs or sipping vinegars are mostly used as a base for a refreshing drink or cocktail. They are a great way to get a second use out of overripe fruit. This recipe uses rhubarb and strawberries, but you can certainly experiment with other flavor combinations.

1 cup (160g) rhubarb, roughly chopped

1 cup (175g) strawberries, stems removed, roughly chopped

1 ¼ (275g) cups white sugar

2 tbsp (15g) ginger, roughly chopped

1 cup (240ml) vinegar of choice (see note)

Instructions

1. In a saucepan on medium heat, combine chopped fruit, ginger, and sugar. Bring to a simmer to dissolve sugar and continue to simmer on low for 10 minutes. The fruit should be mushy and the liquid bright red.

2. Set the saucepan aside to cool completely.

3. Using a fine mesh strainer or a nut milk bag, strain the cooled mixture into a clean bowl. Reserve fruit puree to enjoy with ice cream or in a parfait.

4. Transfer infused syrup to a mason jar and add vinegar. The final product should be both sweet and tart at the same time.

5. Serve on ice with sparkling water, or if you're feeling boozy, add a shot of gin.

Notes: Shrubs will keep in the refrigerator for up to 3 months. I prefer to use a combination of apple cider vinegar and champagne vinegar, but feel free to use what you have on hand.

Snacks & Dips

Burrata and Spring Pesto Toast

A springtime indulgence. This open-face sandwich hits all the wonderful seasonal notes that spring has to offer.

1 thick slice of sourdough bread, toasted

½ ball of burrata (or substitute vegan burrata or vegan mozzarella if desired)

2–3 tbsp (30ml–45ml) Spring Pesto (recipe on page 163)

1 radish, very thinly sliced

Flaky salt

Choice of spring flowers, pea shoots, crushed pistachios, extra-virgin olive oil, and/or herbs for garnish

Instructions

Build up your toast by layering the burrata, pesto, radish slices, flaky salt, and garnish. Drizzle some good quality extra-virgin olive oil on top and enjoy it right away.

Summer Tomato Toast

No introduction is needed. This is my go-to lunch or snack whenever I need a quick tomatoey fix.

1 thick slice of sourdough bread, toasted

1 garlic clove, peeled

1–2 tbsp (15g–30g) mayonnaise (or substitute vegan mayonnaise)

1 tomato, sliced (see note)

Flaky salt, crushed black pepper, and basil leaves for garnish

Instructions

1. While the toasted sourdough bread is still warm, rub it all over with a garlic clove. The ridges in the toast will gently scrape the garlic clove, creating a nice subtle garlicky layer.

2. Slather mayonnaise over toast and arrange sliced tomatoes to your liking.

3. Garnish with flaky salt, fresh cracked pepper, and basil leaves.

Notes: Slicer varieties like Brandywine or Black Beauty are ideal.

Autumn Squash Toast

This autumn toast does take some time to prepare, but I think it's totally worth it! I prefer to make it for large gatherings as a canapé.

Delicata or butternut squash

Extra-virgin olive oil

1 tsp (2g) ground coriander

Kosher salt

2 tbsp (28g) salted butter (or substitute vegan butter)

Sage leaves

2 tbsp (38g) maple syrup

Toasted sliced baguette or sourdough bread

Ricotta (or substitute vegan ricotta product)

Toasted sunflower seeds

Flaky salt

Instructions

1. Preheat your oven to 400°F (200°C).

2. Carefully cut the squash vertically and remove the seeds. Cut each half into semi-circles about ¼" (6mm) thick. Toss in extra-virgin olive oil, ground coriander, and a big pinch of salt.

3. Transfer squash to a baking sheet lined with parchment paper. Bake for 15–20 minutes, or until the squash is tender and slightly caramelized around the edges.

4. While the squash bakes, prepare the fried sage leaves. In a small frying pan, heat 2 tbsp butter until melted. Continue to cook until butter begins to brown (if utilizing vegan ingredients, butter may not brown). Once browned lightly, turn off the heat and add sage leaves to the pan. Careful, there will be splatter. After about 30 seconds, the sage leaves should be crisp. Transfer them to a plate lined with a paper towel and set them aside.

5. Add 2 tbsp of maple syrup to the pan and swirl to combine. Set aside.

6. Assemble the toast by layering ricotta, roasted squash, a drizzle of brown butter maple sauce, and the crispy sage leaves. You can also add some toasted sunflower seeds and/or flaky salt should your heart desire.

Notes: Vegan substitutes currently exist in the market for ricotta. Alternatively, you can omit ricotta altogether and replace it with Autumn Pesto (see recipe on page 165). Delicata squash skin can be eaten, but feel free to peel it before roasting if you choose.

Tomato Tart

Who doesn't love a quick meal that comes together in no time? This puff pastry-based tart is a showstopper and a crowd pleaser. There are so many ways you can make this your own depending on what you have on hand and the season.

1 sheet of frozen puff pastry

¼ cup (60ml) Summer Pesto (recipe on page 164)

¼ cup (55g) shredded mozzarella (or substitute vegan mozzarella)

Mixture of tomatoes, sliced and patted dry (see note)

Thyme sprigs

Kosher salt and fresh cracked pepper to taste

Serves 2–4 people.

Instructions

1. Preheat your oven to 425°F (220°C).

2. Thaw puff pastry as per package instructions and unroll. If using a puff pastry brick, roll out to a rectangle that is 12 inches wide and 15 inches long.

3. Using the tip of a knife, score a ½-inch wide border around the puff pastry sheet. You are essentially drawing a rectangle within a rectangle. Using the tines of a fork, poke the pastry inside the score lines. Make sure to poke evenly and all the way through. We don't want the inner part of the pastry to rise too much, however, we want the border to rise and create a nice crust.

4. Spread the pesto in an even layer without getting any on the border.

5. Sprinkle the shredded mozzarella over the pesto.

6. Arrange the sliced tomatoes over the pesto and cheese mixture. Season to taste. Remember the pesto will be salty so be conservative with your seasoning.

7. Bake for 20–25 minutes. Keep a watchful eye as puff pastry can burn quickly.

8. Once out of the oven, garnish with fresh thyme.

Notes: If using slicer tomatoes, which tend to be juicy and wet when sliced, it's important to allow them to drain slightly before placing them on the tart. Slice tomatoes ¼" (6mm) thick and salt them. Place on paper towels to drain for 15 minutes. Feel free to use basil instead of thyme as garnish. Do your thing! Any leftovers should be stored in the refrigerator and will last for up to 2 days; however, I recommend enjoying this tart while it's warm.

 This recipe was adapted from my popular tomato and herbed cheese puff pastry tart recipe on my blog. Scan the QR code to view the recipe on the blog.

Hummus with Blistered Cherry Tomatoes

A crowd-pleaser, here hummus is amped up with garden goodness, making it so much more special. This recipe is incredibly adaptable, and I encourage you to change up the toppings based on the season and mood.

Hummus

One 19 oz (540ml) can of chickpeas, drained and rinsed

½ cup (120ml) extra-virgin olive oil

¼ cup (60ml) tahini

4–5 tbsp (60ml–75ml) lemon juice

2 garlic cloves, peeled

Kosher salt and fresh cracked pepper to taste

½ tsp (2.5g) cumin (optional)

Topping

1 tbsp (15ml) extra-virgin olive oil

1 cup (150g) cherry tomatoes

Za'atar spice blend

Chopped parsley (optional)

Extra-virgin olive oil to drizzle on just before serving (optional)

Serves 4–6 people.

Instructions

1. In a food processor, place drained and rinsed chickpeas, olive oil, tahini, lemon juice, garlic, kosher salt, black pepper, and cumin. Process and scrape the sides down.

2. Because lemons have varying levels of juice, you may need to add more lemon juice to taste. If the hummus is too thick, add more olive oil to loosen it up.

3. Process until very smooth. When you think you're done processing, process for another 60 seconds. Trust me, this is how you get creamy and unctuous hummus.

4. Taste and adjust seasoning.

5. Spread hummus in a bowl or on a plate.

6. In a small frying pan, add cherry tomatoes to 1 tbsp extra-virgin olive oil. Cook on high heat until tomatoes start to blister and pop but not fall apart. This should only take 3–5 minutes, depending on your stovetop.

7. Spoon warm cherry tomatoes over hummus.

8. Sprinkle Za'atar spice blend over the top. Use as much or as little as you like. Sprinkle chopped parsley if using. Drizzle extra-virgin olive oil if using. Enjoy with pita or crackers.

Notes: Homemade hummus will keep in the refrigerator for up to 3 days. It is best enjoyed fresh. If you must, you can make it ahead by one day and store it in an airtight container until you need to serve it. For an extra special occasion, boil the drained canned chickpeas in water for 10 minutes to help release the skins. Rinse under cold water and pick out the chickpea skins and discard them. Continue with the recipe as outlined. This step will yield the creamiest hummus ever, but it's completely optional.

Mutabal (Charred Eggplant Dip)

Growing up, my mother made this appetizer with oven-roasted eggplants. I prefer fire-roasted eggplant as this gives the final dish a smoky aroma and flavor. However, since fire roasting isn't a suitable option for most, this recipe will showcase my mother's tried-and-true oven-roasted method. Mutabal is often confused with baba ghanoush. Traditionally speaking, they are different. Mutabal recipes typically include tahini, whereas baba ghanoush recipes shouldn't. But over the years and for various reasons, that distinction has faded and the recipes have morphed into a hybrid of sorts.

1 large Italian eggplant
(or two medium)

1–2 garlic cloves, grated
or finely minced

2–3 tbsp (30ml–45ml) tahini

2 tbsp (30ml) lemon juice

1 tsp (5g) cumin (optional)

Kosher salt and fresh
cracked pepper to taste

Optional Garnish

Mixture of fresh herbs
(I recommend mint and parsley)

Pomegranate seeds

Aleppo pepper

Sumac

Extra-virgin olive oil

Serves 4–6 people.

Instructions

1. Cut the eggplant vertically down the middle and rub the cut parts with a sprinkle of kosher salt and olive oil. Roast cut side down on a parchment-lined baking sheet for 20–30 minutes at 400ºF (200ºC). Eggplant will be ready when the skin collapses and the flesh is soft. Cool for 15 minutes before proceeding with the next step.

2. Scrape the flesh into a fine-mesh sieve placed over a bowl. Allow eggplant flesh to drain for 30–60 minutes. Discard liquid.

3. Add eggplant flesh to a bowl, and mash with a fork. Add garlic, tahini, lemon juice, and cumin if using. Add salt and pepper to taste. Add more garlic or lemon juice if you desire.

4. Plate the eggplant dip in a shallow bowl or a rimmed plate and top with all or some of the garnish options listed. Olive oil is a must. Serve with pita, crackers, and/or crudités.

Notes: Mutabal will keep in the refrigerator for up to 3 days. It is best enjoyed fresh. If you must, you can make it one day ahead and store it in an airtight container until you need to serve it. My mother will often add 2 tablespoons of yogurt to the mix, which makes the final product richer in taste and lighter in color.

If you're inclined to try preparing a fire-roasted version of this recipe, scan the QR code to view the recipe and instructions on the blog.

Cucumber Yogurt Dip

Recipes from the Mediterranean region are steeped in a rich history. There is incredible overlap in what you would consider Greek, Turkish, Persian, or Middle Eastern Cuisine. Take Tzatziki for example. The Turks have a version called Cacık (which is runnier and includes dried mint). The Persians have Mast-o Khiar (oftentimes including walnuts and/or raisins). The Levantines have Khyar Bi Laban (a dish quite similar to traditional Greek Tzatziki, but without the dill). We are all much more alike than we'd like to admit. This recipe is adapted from my mother's Khyar Bi Laban recipe and a traditional Tzatziki.

3 Persian cucumbers, grated

1 cup (245g) Greek yogurt (or substitute vegan yogurt)

2 tbsp (3g) fresh mint, finely chopped (or 1 tbsp dried mint)

1 tbsp (3g) fresh dill, finely chopped

2 garlic cloves, finely minced

1 tbsp (15ml) lemon juice

Kosher salt and fresh cracked pepper to taste

Extra-virgin olive oil and Shattah for garnish, optional (recipe on page 197)

Serves 2–4 people.

Instructions

1. Squeeze the grated cucumber by hand or in a clean tea towel. Discard (or reserve) liquid—see note.

2. In a bowl, add grated and squeezed cucumber, yogurt, mint, dill, garlic and lemon juice. Stir to combine. Season to taste.

3. Transfer to a serving plate; drizzle with extra-virgin olive oil and top with shattah, if using.

Notes: This dip will keep in the refrigerator for 2–3 days; any longer and it will begin to separate. For vegan preparations, use a thick Greek-style vegan yogurt. Coconut yogurt can also be used. Cucumber liquid can be added to lemonades or cocktails or enjoyed on its own.

Roasted Tomatillo Salsa Verde

This tangy, herbaceous, spicy, and satisfying salsa is the only reason why I grow tomatillos. It can be enjoyed on its own with chips or drizzled on tacos, fajitas, huevos rancheros, and a host of other dishes.

1 lb. (450g) fresh tomatillos (about 8–12 fruits), husks removed and fruits cleaned

1 white onion, peeled and halved

2–4 hot green peppers such as jalapeño, serrano, or any hot green variety

4 garlic cloves, skin on

Fresh cilantro, more or less to taste

2 tbsp (30ml) white distilled vinegar

2 tbsp (30ml) lime juice

Kosher salt and fresh cracked pepper to taste

Ground cumin to taste (optional)

Instructions

1. Using a cast iron pan set on medium-high heat, dry roast the tomatillos, onion halves, peppers, and garlic. We want some scorch marks but not to cook the ingredients. This should take 4–6 minutes. Keep flipping ingredients to get charring on multiple sides. Alternatively, you can broil the ingredients in your oven, which can take up to 10 minutes.

2. Carefully peel the dry roasted garlic and place in the blender along with the scorched tomatillos and onion halves.

3. If you like your salsa spicy, add the hot peppers whole. If you prefer a milder sauce, remove the seeds and discard them. If you're not sure how spicy it will be, start with one hot pepper. You can always add heat to a sauce, but you cannot take it out without diluting it.

4. Add the cilantro, lime juice, white vinegar, ½ tsp salt, a few grinds of pepper, and cumin (if using),

5. Pulse the blender for 20–30 seconds. Blend on low/medium, but don't over-process.

6. Taste your sauce and adjust seasonings.

7. Pulse or process to desired consistency. I like it a little chunky.

Notes: Store your salsa in mason jars or glass containers. Avoid any metal containers. The salsa will keep in the fridge for up to a week. If you intend to freeze your salsa, I recommend you cook it down to remove some of the water content. Transfer the salsa to a small saucepan and cook on medium heat for 8–10 minutes. Let it cool, then transfer to mason jars or deli containers and freeze. Frozen green salsa will keep for up to one year, but I guarantee you'll use it before then.

One of my favorite ways to amp this salsa up is by adding grilled or ripe summer peaches. The end result is a sweet, tangy, spicy sauce that pairs well with an array of proteins and vegetables. Scan the QR code to see this recipe variation on the blog.

Stuffed Squash Blossoms

A summertime classic. Did you know that most parts of the zucchini plant are edible, including the leaves and the flowers? Personally, I have no interest in eating zucchini foliage, but the flowers are a must. This is a classic ricotta-stuffed and fried squash blossom recipe, but with a sweet twist.

1 cup (250g) ricotta (or substitute vegan ricotta or cream cheese product)

¼ cup (25g) grated Parmigiano Reggiano (or substitute 2 tbsp nutritional yeast)

¼ cup (55g) shredded mozzarella (or substitute vegan mozzarella)

Pinch of nutmeg

Kosher salt and fresh cracked pepper to taste

8–10 squash blossoms (see note)

½ cup (60g) all-purpose flour

2 tbsp (16g) corn starch

¾ cup (175ml) seltzer water (see note)

Vegetable oil for frying

Chopped chives, flaky salt, and honey (or substitute agave nectar or maple syrup) for garnish

Serves 2–4 people.

Instructions

1. Prepare the stuffing mixture by combining ricotta, Parmigiano Reggiano, shredded mozzarella, nutmeg, salt, and pepper. **Optional:** Transfer the mixture to a small piping bag.

2. Carefully pry open the squash blossom without tearing and spoon (or pipe) in 1–2 tbsp of filling. Twist the tips of the blossom to seal the mixture in. Do not overstuff the blossoms. A little filling goes a long way.

3. In a medium-sized bowl, combine flour and cornstarch. Slowly drizzle seltzer water into the bowl while whisking continuously until you reach a loose pancake batter consistency.

4. In a large frying pan, add enough oil to reach a depth of ¼" (6mm). Set the heat to medium.

5. Test the oil by dropping some batter in. If it begins to sizzle, the oil is ready.

6. Carefully dip stuffed blossoms in the batter, allowing any excess to drip off. Shallow fry on each side for approximately 2 minutes.

7. Transfer fried blossoms to a tray or plate lined with paper towels to drain for a few minutes.

8. Plate fried squash blossoms and garnish with chives, flaky salt, and a drizzle of honey.

Notes: Both male and female squash blossoms are edible. I recommend snipping off and discarding the stigma or stamen using a pair of scissors before stuffing the flowers. Be careful, squash pollen can stain. Seltzer water or club soda is an ideal liquid for the batter as it creates a fluffier and less dense final product. You certainly could use a light beer instead. Shallow frying is recommended for this recipe. These fried squash blossoms should be enjoyed right away as they don't stay crunchy for long.

Salads

Herbaceous Lettuce and Radish Salad

Lettuces and radishes tend to mature around the same time. My first salad of the growing season will typically feature lettuce, radish, and the first clippings of delicate herbs from my perennial herb patch.

1–2 heads of a delicate lettuce such as bibb or butterhead, leaves separated, washed, and spun dry

6–8 radishes, trimmed and thinly sliced

3 tbsp (20g) walnuts, roughly chopped

3 tbsp (9g) chives, cut into 1" (2cm) strips

3 tbsp (4g) mint, roughly chopped

Shaved Parmigiano Reggiano (optional)

Dressing

¼ cup (60ml) extra-virgin olive oil

2 tbsp (30ml) red wine vinegar

2 tbsp (6g) chives, roughly chopped

1 tsp (5ml) Dijon mustard

1 tsp (7g) honey or maple syrup

Kosher salt and fresh cracked pepper to taste

Serves 2–4. Scale up or down as needed.

Instructions

1. In a mason jar, combine extra-virgin olive oil, red wine vinegar, chives, Dijon mustard, and honey (or maple syrup). Using an immersion blender, process until you get a smooth and emulsified dressing. Season to taste.

2. On a serving platter, layer lettuce leaves and radish slices. Drizzle on as much or as little dressing as you would like. Garnish with walnuts, chives, mint, and shaved Parmigiano Reggiano.

Notes: This salad is best enjoyed right away and works well as a counterbalance to a heavy or greasy meal. The dressing can be made a day ahead. Assemble before serving.

Maha's Chopped Salad

No matter the meal at hand, this salad always graced my mother's dining table. It's simple, delicious, and quite nutritious. Many cultures claim ownership over this classic salad. Some trace the origin back to the Ottoman Empire, others claim that it's Persian. I just know it as Maha's chopped salad, and it's just perfect when the garden is pumping out fresh, vine-ripened tomatoes and crisp juicy cucumbers.

5 Persian cucumbers (or 1 English cucumber)

4 ripe plum tomatoes

1 red bell pepper

3 spring onions

¼ cup (5g) flatleaf parsley

¼ cup (5g) fresh mint

2 tbsp (30ml) lemon juice

¼ cup (60ml) extra-virgin olive oil

2 tbsp (30ml) red wine vinegar

Kosher salt and fresh cracked pepper to taste

Serves 6–8. Scale up or down as needed.

Instructions

1. Quarter cucumbers lengthwise. Remove and discard seeds by slicing away the cavity. Chop into small ¼" (6mm) cubes and add to a large bowl.

2. Slice tomatoes and dice into ¼" (6mm) cubes, then add them to the bowl. If the tomatoes you are using are extra juicy, remove and discard the seed cavity. Otherwise, the salad may be too watery.

3. Dice red bell pepper and spring onion into ¼" (6mm) chunks and add to the bowl.

4. Chop parsley and mint as finely as possible and add to the bowl.

5. Add lemon juice, olive oil, and red wine vinegar. Season with 1 tsp of kosher salt and a few grinds of black pepper to start.

6. Mix well, taste, and adjust the seasoning.

Notes: This salad is best enjoyed right away. If you must make it ahead, reserve the olive oil, lemon, and vinegar, and add them to the salad right before serving. Enjoy as a side with grilled vegetables and proteins. This salad is an excellent base recipe that can be adapted in several ways. Add kalamata olive, cubed feta, and some dried oregano for a Greek twist on this classic Middle Eastern salad. Add a can of mixed beans or red kidney beans and you have yourself a hearty bean salad for your next picnic.

Beet, Feta, and Herb Salad

One of my mom's classics, but with a twist. My mother's herby beet salad was a frequent fixture on our dinner table. I have taken her recipe and added pistachios for crunch and feta for a tangy bite. The result is a well-balanced salad that covers all five tastes: sweet, bitter, sour, salty, and umami.

4–5 beets, cleaned and with tops removed

Extra-virgin olive oil for roasting

¼ cup (5g) dill, roughly chopped

¼ cup (5g) mint, roughly chopped

¼ cup (5g) parsley, roughly chopped

½ cup (130g) feta, crumbled (or substitute vegan feta)

¼ cup (38g) pistachios, roughly chopped (optional)

Dressing

¼ cup (60ml) extra-virgin olive oil

2 tbsp (30ml) red wine vinegar

1 tbsp (15ml) lemon juice

1 tsp (5ml) Dijon mustard

1 tsp honey (7g), maple syrup, or agave nectar

Kosher salt and fresh cracked pepper to taste

Serves 2–4. Scale up or down as needed.

Instructions

1. Place the beets on a sheet of aluminum foil; drizzle with 1 tbsp of olive oil and ½ tsp kosher salt, coating the beets evenly. Wrap foil around the beets to create a sealed parcel. Bake at 375°F (190°C) for 30–45 minutes; time will vary depending on the size of the beets. To check doneness, insert a knife through a beet. If you don't meet resistance, they are ready. Allow the beets to cool, remove the skins, and cut them into wedges or disks.

2. Add all dressing ingredients to a mason jar and shake vigorously to combine.

3. In a large bowl, add the sliced roasted beets, dill, mint, and parsley, crumbled feta. Toss to combine. Dress with as much or as little dressing as you like.

4. Transfer dressed beets to a serving dish and garnish with optional pistachios.

Notes: This salad can be prepared a day ahead, however, keep the dressing on the side and add it just before serving.

Peach Panzanella-Style Salad

I cannot get enough of Panzanella, a Tuscan summer salad. This version pays homage to the classic by combining fresh heirloom tomatoes with ripe peaches and chunky croutons. It's a perfect side for any family get-together, barbecue, or picnic.

4–5 medium tomatoes, cut into wedges

1 tsp (5g) kosher salt (for tomatoes, see Step 1 below)

3–4 peaches, cut into wedges

2 thick slices of stale bread, cut into 1" (2cm) cubes

Handful of basil leaves, torn by hand.

1 shallot or ½ red onion, thinly sliced

Dressing

¼ cup (60ml) extra-virgin olive oil

2 tbsp (30ml) sherry vinegar or white balsamic vinegar

1 garlic clove, minced

Kosher salt and fresh cracked pepper to taste

Serves 6–8. Scale up or down as needed.

Instructions

1. In a bowl, combine sliced tomatoes and 1 tsp kosher salt. Set aside for 15 minutes. This will draw out the water and make the tomatoes more flavorful. Discard liquid.

2. To the same bowl, add sliced peaches, bread, torn basil, and sliced shallots or onions. Combine.

3. In a mason jar or small bowl, combine dressing ingredients and mix well. Start with just ½ tsp of kosher salt and a few grinds of black pepper.

4. Add dressing to salad and toss.

5. Taste and adjust seasoning to your liking.

Notes: This salad can be prepared a day ahead, however, keep the dressing on the side and add it just before serving. I highly recommend using sherry vinegar as its sharp pungency offsets the sweetness of the peaches quite well. Not quite peach season? You can substitute nectarines or apricots for the peaches.

Roasted Beet and Zucchini Salad

In my garden, the beet harvest begins when the zucchini vines begin fruiting. This salad should be served warm or at room temperature for optimal flavor and texture.

2–3 large beets, peeled and cubed into ½" (1cm) pieces (see note)

1 zucchini, quartered lengthwise, seed cavity removed and cubed into ½" (1cm) pieces

1 large eggplant (or 2 Asian long eggplants), cubed into ½" (1cm) pieces

Extra-virgin olive oil for roasting

1 cup (185g) cooked fregola pasta (see note for substitutions)

1 cup (260g) feta, crumbled into large chunks (or substitute vegan feta)

3 spring onions, finely chopped

¼ cup (5g) parsley, roughly chopped

¼ cup (5g) dill, roughly chopped

2 tbsp (2.5g) mint, roughly chopped

Dressing

¼ cup (60ml) extra-virgin olive oil

2 tbsp (30ml) red wine vinegar

1 tbsp (15ml) maple syrup

1 tsp (5ml) Dijon mustard

Kosher salt and fresh cracked pepper to taste

Serves 6–8. Scale up or down as needed.

Instructions

1. Preheat your oven to 350°F (175°C). On a baking tray lined with parchment paper, toss the cubed beetroot with a drizzle of olive oil and about ½ tsp of kosher salt. Roast at 350°F (175°C).

2. After 15 minutes, remove the tray from the oven and carefully add the cubed zucchini and eggplant. Toss with the half-cooked beetroots and place the tray back in the oven for another 20 minutes.

3. After a total of 35 minutes of baking, the beetroot, zucchini, and eggplant should be fork-tender. If not, cook for an additional 5–10 minutes. While the roasted vegetables cool, proceed with the rest of the steps.

4. In a large serving bowl, prepare your dressing. Combine extra-virgin olive oil, red wine vinegar, maple syrup, ½ tsp of kosher salt to start, and a good grind of black pepper. Whisk to emulsify.

5. To the same bowl, add roasted vegetables, cooked and cooled fregola, crumbled feta, green onions, and herbs. Toss to combine. Taste and adjust seasoning as desired.

Notes: I recommend using gloves when peeling and cutting the beets to avoid staining (or choose golden beets instead as they are more forgiving). Fregola is a type of pasta from Sardinia. You can use quinoa, barley, faro, orzo, canned beans, or even chickpeas instead of the fregola to cater to your taste, allergies, and preferences. This salad is very adaptable and can be made with a range of vegetables you may have on hand. It holds up well and can be stored in the refrigerator for up to 3 days.

Pestos & Sauces

Spring Pesto (Peas and Pistachios)

As much as I love traditional Genovese pesto, the king of pesto, I do enjoy taking some creative liberties through the season depending on what's available in the garden. This pea and mint pesto is a gift to your tastebuds after a long winter.

1 cup (135g) fresh peas

½ cup (10g) arugula, packed

½ cup (10g) fresh mint leaves, packed

¼ cup (38g) pistachios

¼ cup (25g) grated Parmigiano Reggiano (sub. 2 tbsp nutritional yeast)

1–2 garlic cloves, peeled

¼ cup (60ml) extra-virgin olive oil

1 tbsp (15ml) lemon juice

Kosher salt and fresh cracked pepper to taste

Instructions

1. In a small pot, bring water to a boil and add the peas. Cook for 1–2 minutes until the peas are tender.

2. To the same pot, add the arugula and mint. Wait 30 seconds, strain in a colander, and rinse under cold water. This blanching process helps preserve the color after processing.

3. Transfer cooled peas, arugula, and mint to a food processor. Add the pistachios, Parmigiano Reggiano (or nutritional yeast), garlic, olive oil, and lemon juice. Process to desired consistency. Taste and adjust seasoning.

Notes: Store in the fridge in an airtight container for up to 3 days. Alternatively, freeze in a deli container or freezer bag for up to 6 months.

Summer Pesto (Basil and Walnut)

Though the addition of walnuts may bother Genovese pesto purists, I stand by my more attainable and affordable nut choice. Pine nuts are however traditional; by all means, feel free to use them instead of walnuts if you can find a reliable source of European pine nuts.

2 cups (50g) packed basil leaves

½ cup (60g) walnuts

½ cup (50g) grated Parmigiano Reggiano (or substitute 2 tbsp nutritional yeast)

¼ cup (60ml) extra-virgin olive oil

1 tbsp (15ml) lemon juice

1–2 garlic cloves, peeled

Kosher salt and fresh cracked pepper to taste

Instructions

1. **Optional Step:** In a pot of boiling water, blanch basil for 30 seconds. Using a slotted spoon, transfer blanched basil leaves to a bowl of ice water. Using your hands, remove the basil from the ice bath and squeeze out as much water as possible. Set aside.

2. In a food processor, add the walnuts, grated Parmigiano Reggiano (or nutritional yeast), extra-virgin olive oil, lemon juice, and garlic. Process until you have a coarse wet mixture.

3. Add the basil to the food processor and continue to process until you reach your desired consistency.

4. Taste and adjust your seasonings. Parmigiano Reggiano is salty, so you may not need to add much salt.

Notes: Store pesto in an airtight jar in the fridge for up to 3 days. Cover the pesto with a thin layer of oil to help prevent oxidation. Alternatively, you can freeze your pesto in deli containers or reusable glass containers. Use within 6 months. **A note on pine nuts:** Some people may experience "pine mouth," a condition that presents itself as a metallic taste in the mouth that can last for several days or more. This is why I personally prefer to use walnuts.

Autumn Pesto (Kale and Almond)

When the weather cools and garden kale is less bitter, it can be transformed into a hearty pesto that will pair well with pasta, eggs, or proteins.

2 cups (135g) packed chopped kale leaves (discard stems)

½ cup (75g) toasted almonds

½ cup (50g) grated Parmigiano Reggiano (or substitute 2 tbsp nutritional yeast)

¼ cup (60ml) extra-virgin olive oil

½ lemon, juiced and zested

1–2 garlic cloves, peeled

Kosher salt and fresh cracked pepper to taste

Crushed pepper flakes (optional)

Instructions

1. In a pot of boiling water, blanch the kale for 60 seconds. Using a slotted spoon, transfer the blanched kale leaves to a bowl of ice water. Once cooled, squeeze out as much water as possible from the blanched kale and set it aside.

2. In a food processor, add the almonds, grated Parmigiano Reggiano (or nutritional yeast), extra-virgin olive oil, lemon zest, lemon juice, garlic, and crushed pepper flakes if using. Process until you have a coarse wet mixture.

3. Add the blanched kale to the food processor and continue to process until you reach your desired consistency.

4. Taste and adjust your seasonings. Parmigiano Reggiano is salty, so you may not need to add much salt.

Notes: Store pesto in an airtight jar in the fridge for up to 3 days. Cover the pesto with a thin layer of oil to help prevent oxidation. Alternatively, you can freeze your pesto in deli containers or reusable glass containers. Use within 6 months.

Roasted Tomato Sauce

The Mother Sauce; this is more of a method than a recipe, and the end result can be used in many different ways. When summer tomatoes are coming in hot and heavy, I transform the harvest into this sauce that I can then freeze in a pinch.

3–4 lbs. (1.3kg–1.8kg) fresh paste or slicer tomatoes, cut in half

4–5 garlic cloves, peeled

¼ cup (60ml) extra-virgin olive oil

Choice of herbs

1 large onion, peeled and cut in half (optional)

Kosher salt and fresh cracked pepper to taste

Instructions

1. Preheat your oven to 375°F (190°C).

2. On a rimmed baking tray lined with parchment paper, place the tomatoes, garlic cloves, and onion halves (if using) in a single layer. Drizzle with olive oil and sprinkle with a few pinches of kosher salt. Tuck herb sprigs around the tomatoes.

3. Roast for 30–45 minutes. If your tomatoes are particularly juicy, you may need to roast them for 15 minutes longer.

4. Remove the tray from the oven when tomatoes look roasted and have shrunk slightly. Cool for 30 minutes before proceeding. Discard the herbs.

5. Transfer the roasted tomatoes, garlic, and onions to a blender or food processor. Process until desired consistency is reached. Taste and adjust seasoning.

6. If you feel the sauce is still too watery for your liking, transfer to a saucepan and simmer uncovered on low to medium heat until you reach the desired consistency.

7. Cool, transfer to mason jars, and refrigerate.

Notes: If you prefer a silky-smooth sauce, run it through a fine-mesh strainer before storing. This sauce will keep in the fridge for up to 5 days. I like to freeze it in deli containers and use it throughout the winter months. Feel free to play around with the flavor profile. Try different herb combinations, or add a hot pepper for a fiery sauce.

 It can be daunting to eat and process all the tomatoes (especially cherry tomatoes) your garden is pumping out at the peak of summer. For ideas on how you can enjoy and process them, scan the QR code to read a blog post on this topic.

Larger Dishes

Risotto with Spring Greens and Asparagus

What I appreciate about risotto is that it can be a blank canvas for your imagination to shine. It's also the perfect canvas for seasonal eating. This recipe focuses on springtime staples like spinach and asparagus, which will typically be in season around the same time. Apply the same technique outlined in this recipe throughout the year and let the seasons guide you.

5–7 cups (1.1L–1.6L) of a broth of your choice

2 tbsp (30ml) extra-virgin olive oil

3 garlic cloves, finely minced

2 shallots (or 1 onion), finely minced

3 thyme sprigs

1½ cups (330g) short grain Arborio rice

½ cup (120ml) white vermouth or dry white wine (optional)

3–4 cups (90g–120g) chopped fresh spinach

1 cup (125g) asparagus, trimmed and cut at an angle into 1" (2cm) pieces

1 lemon, zested

3 tbsp (45ml) lemon juice

½ cup (50g) grated Parmigiano Reggiano (or substitute 2 tbsp nutritional yeast)

Kosher salt and fresh cracked pepper to taste

Chives, Parmigiano Reggiano, burrata, and/or spring pesto for garnish

Serves 4–6 people.

Instructions

1. In a pot, bring broth up to a simmer.

2. In a heavy bottom pot, add extra-virgin olive oil, minced garlic, minced shallots, and thyme. Season with a big pinch of salt and a few grinds of black pepper. Sautee on medium-high heat until translucent, about 4–6 minutes. Do not let garlic brown; reduce heat if necessary.

3. Add the Arborio rice and toss to coat with the oil and aromatics. Keep stirring for 3–4 minutes. Toasting the Arborio rice slightly brings out some of its nutty flavor.

4. Reduce the heat to medium-low. Add the vermouth or wine (if using) to deglaze the pot. With a wooden spoon, stir and carefully scrape the bottom of the pan to release all the flavorful bits. Continue stirring until the vermouth is absorbed.

5. Pour the broth over the rice one ladleful at a time, making sure the broth is absorbed between additions. It is important to take this step slowly as this method creates a creamy finished product. This can take anywhere from 20–40 minutes.

6. Taste your rice. At this point, it should be cooked through but still *al dente* (a slight bite in the center). Remove thyme sprigs.

7.   Add spinach, asparagus, lemon zest, and lemon juice. Continue to stir for 2–4 minutes, until spinach is wilted and asparagus is cooked.

8.   Turn the heat off and add Parmigiano Reggiano (or nutritional yeast). Taste and adjust seasoning.

9.   Serve warm adorned with fresh chives, a few dollops of spring pesto, some burrata, and more Parmigiano Reggiano if you wish.

Notes: Risotto should be prepared right before serving. Leftovers can be stored in the fridge for up to 3 days. Get creative and try different flavor combinations. Squash and basil work well together; so do mushrooms and peas.

Curried Lentils and Greens

This lentil coconut curry is one of my go-to recipes, and it comes together pretty quickly using staple pantry ingredients. It is satisfyingly hearty, and it is inherently vegan. As a child growing up in the Middle East, I was exposed to recipes and the taste of foods from India, Sri Lanka, and Pakistan. These spices and flavors have been prevalent in Middle Eastern dishes for centuries largely because of the spice trade routes that ran from the Indian subcontinent through the Arab world and on into Europe. This recipe is in many ways a fusion of Southeast Asian, Indian, and Middle Eastern flavors.

2 tbsp (30ml) vegetable oil

1 onion, finely chopped

2–3 garlic cloves, finely chopped

2 tbsp (15g) ginger, finely minced

1 tsp (3g) ground turmeric

1 tsp (3g) ground cumin

1 tsp (2g) ground coriander

½ tsp (2.5g) ground cinnamon

1 cup (210g) red lentils, cleaned and picked over (see note)

2–3 cups (475ml–700ml) vegetable broth

1 can (400ml) coconut milk

3–4 cups (90g–120g) greens, chopped (use spinach, chard, and/or kale)

2 tbsp (30ml) lime juice

Kosher salt and fresh cracked pepper to taste

Cilantro, coconut milk, and hot sauce for garnish

Serves 2–4 people.

Instructions

1. In a pot, heat vegetable oil and add chopped onion, garlic, and ginger. Sautee on medium heat until translucent and fragrant, about 2–3 minutes. Add turmeric, cumin, coriander, and cinnamon. Stir to combine. Continue stirring for 1–2 minutes until spices toast. If you find the bottom of the pot starting to scorch, lower the heat and add a splash of water.

2. To the pot, add rinsed red lentils and 2 cups of broth. Stir well, making sure to scrape up any bits from the bottom of the pot (that's where the flavor is). Bring to a gentle simmer and cook for 10 minutes.

3. Add the coconut milk (reserving ¼ cup for garnish) and continue to simmer until the curry is thick and creamy and the lentils are cooked. Add more broth if needed.

4. Add chopped greens and fold in gently. The greens will wilt and release some water. Continue to cook until desired consistency is reached.

5. Add lime juice. Season with kosher salt and fresh cracked pepper to taste. Garnish with fresh cilantro leaves, reserved coconut milk, and hot sauce.

6. Serve with rice, fresh naan, and lime wedges.

Stuffed Eggplant

Is there a flavor combination that's been etched in your mind since childhood? For me, it's my mother's ground meat mixture with toasted pine nuts and *bharat*, a Levantine seven spice blend that includes coriander, cumin, cinnamon, allspice, nutmeg, cloves, and black pepper. This spice blend can be purchased at all Middle Eastern stores, but you don't really need it. You can use staple pantry spices as outlined below to achieve a similar flavor profile.

2 large Italian eggplants

2 tbsp (30ml) extra-virgin olive oil, divided

Kosher salt

1 large onion, finely diced

3–4 garlic cloves, finely diced

1 tbsp (5g) ground coriander

1 tbsp (8g) ground cumin

½ tsp (2.5g) cinnamon

½ tsp (2.5g) crushed chili flakes

1 lb. (450g) ground meat or alternative (see note)

¼ cup (35g) pine nuts, plus extra for garnish

2 cups (475ml) Roasted Tomato Sauce (recipe on page 167), or you can use canned crushed tomatoes

2 tbsp (2.5g) parsley, finely chopped

Kosher salt and fresh cracked pepper to taste

Tahini Sauce

¼ cup (60ml) tahini

1 tbsp (15ml) lemon juice

Cold water

Kosher salt and fresh ground pepper to taste

Serves 2–4 people.

Instructions

1. Preheat your oven to 400°F (200°C) and line a baking sheet with parchment paper. Slice the eggplants vertically and brush cut ends with extra-virgin olive oil (1 tbsp). Season with a pinch of salt. Bake cut side up for 20–25 minutes, or until the flesh is soft, but not fully cooked through.

2. While the eggplants are baking, prepare the filling mixture. In a frying pan on medium heat, add 1 tbsp extra-virgin olive oil, onions, and garlic. Fry for 3–4 minutes until onions are translucent.

3. Add the ground coriander, cumin, cinnamon, and chili flakes and sauté for 2 minutes until fragrant.

4. Add ground meat mixture along with ½ tsp of salt and a few grinds of black pepper. Continue to fry, stirring regularly to break up any large chunks, until fully cooked. This should take anywhere between 5–8 minutes.

5. Add the pine nuts; stir well and continue to fry for another 1–2 minutes.

6. Add the tomato sauce or crushed tomatoes. Continue to cook, stirring to combine, until mixture thickens slightly (about 5–8 minutes).

7. Add the chopped parsley, taste, and adjust the seasoning.

8. After 20 minutes in the oven, remove the baking sheet. Create a slit vertically down each eggplant half using a sharp knife, taking extra care not to cut all the way down to the skin below. Using 2 spoons, carefully pry open this slit to create a pocket.

9. Divide the stuffing mixture equally among the eggplants and return the tray to the oven. Reduce the temperature to 350°F (175°C) and bake for another 15–20 minutes.

10. While the stuffed eggplants bake, prepare the tahini sauce. In a small bowl, whisk together tahini and lemon juice. This will cause the tahini to thicken. Add a tablespoon or two of cold water and continue to whisk until you reach a runny consistency. Season with salt and pepper to taste.

11. Remove the tray. Garnish eggplants with tahini sauce, toasted pine nuts, fresh parsley, and lemon wedges. Serve with rice.

Notes: Traditionally, this recipe is prepared with ground lamb; however, you can certainly use a vegan ground meat alternative or crumbled tofu. Depending on the size of the eggplants you are using, you may need to adjust the baking time. Use your best judgment.

Pasta alla Norma

A Sicilian classic. When I first tried pasta alla Norma, for me, it had a very familiar and comforting flavor profile. After all, Sicily's cuisine is heavily influenced by Arab, Turkish, and Greek food. This is a wonderfully flavorful and hearty recipe that I make often at midsummer, when tomatoes, eggplants, and basil are at their peak.

¼ cup (60ml) olive oil, plus more as needed

1 large globe eggplant, cut into 1" (2.5cm) cubes

Kosher salt

2 garlic cloves, minced

Pinch of chili flakes

1 tsp (1g) dried oregano

Kosher salt and fresh cracked pepper to taste

2 cups (475ml) diced tomatoes or 1 ½ cups (350ml) Roasted Tomato Sauce (recipe on page 167)

½ cup (10g) basil leaves, chopped into strips

12 oz (340g) of your choice of pasta; I prefer rigatoni or penne

Grated ricotta salata or pecorino Romano (or substitute vegan parmesan) for garnish

Serves 4–6 people.

Instructions

1. Add oil to a large sauté pan or Dutch oven and warm on medium heat. Carefully place cubed eggplant in oil, lightly salt, and shallow fry until golden on all sides, about 5–7 minutes. Using a slotted spoon, transfer cooked eggplant to a plate lined with paper towels and set aside. You may need to do this process in batches to avoid crowding the pan.

2. Once all the eggplant has been fried, use the same pan to prepare the sauce. If the pan is dry, add a tablespoon of olive oil. Bring the pan up to medium-low heat and sauté the garlic and chili flakes for 1–2 minutes, stirring constantly to avoid scorching.

3. Add the tomatoes (or tomato sauce) and oregano. Cook the sauce down to your desired consistency. Season to taste. **Note:** If using roasted tomato sauce, you do not need to cook the sauce down. Simply warm through.

4. Cook your pasta in salted hot water, reserving some of the cooking liquid.

5. Transfer the cooked pasta to the sauce pot, along with the fried eggplant and basil leaves. Stir well to combine.

6. Serve with grated ricotta salata or pecorino Romano.

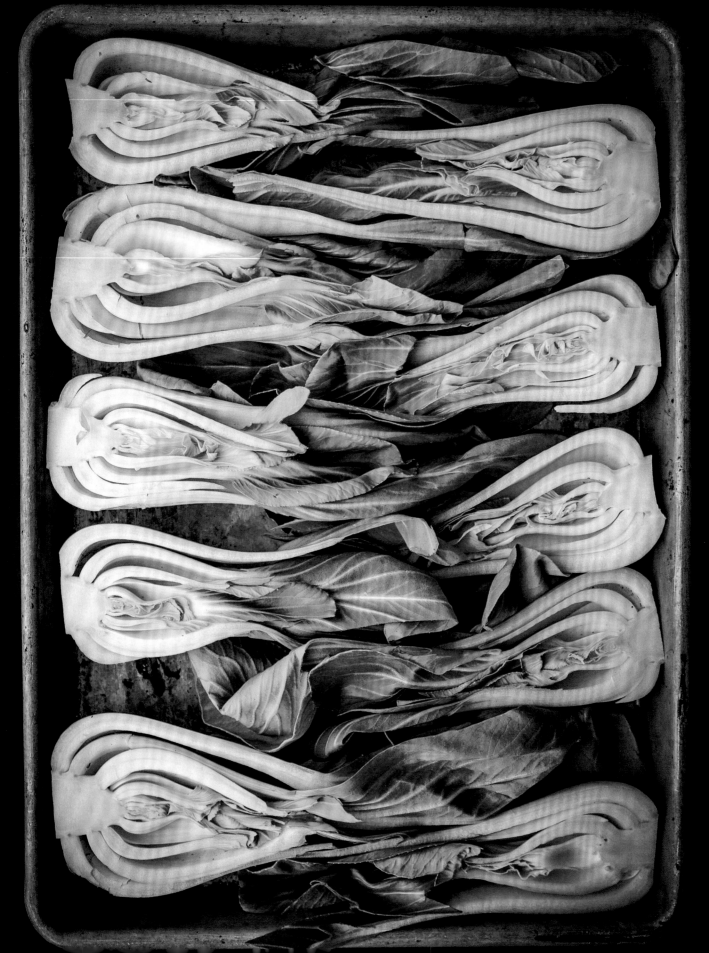

Side Dishes

Smashed Potatoes with Ají

Potatoes might just be the most versatile vegetable out there. The perfect roasted potato for me must include soft buttery flesh with crispy and crunchy edges. This recipe hits all the textural and flavor notes.

1.5 lbs. (700g) new potatoes (see note)

2 tbsp (30ml) olive oil

1 tsp (5g) garlic powder

1 tsp (5g) smoked paprika

1 tsp (5g) kosher salt

Ají (recipe on page 196)

Feta cheese (optional)

Serves 2–4 people.

Instructions

1. Preheat your oven to 375°F (190°C).

2. On a parchment paper-lined baking sheet, combine potatoes, garlic powder, smoked paprika, salt, and olive oil. Toss to coat; roast for 25–35 minutes, or until potatoes are cooked through. Test doneness by inserting a knife into one of the potatoes. You shouldn't meet any resistance.

3. Remove the baking sheet from the oven and crank the heat up to 450°F (230°C).

4. Using the bottom of a heavy drinking glass or plate, gently smash each potato down to a thickness of ½" (1cm). You're looking to crack the skin and expose some of the inner flesh.

5. Return the baking sheet to the hot oven and roast for another 10–15 minutes, or until the smashed potatoes crisp up.

6. When ready, transfer the smashed potatoes to a serving dish. Drizzle with ají and garnish with feta, if using.

Notes: You can also use fingerling or standard potatoes, however, in my experience, new potatoes perform best.

Green Beans with Coriander and Garlic

Freshly harvested string beans are delicious on their own with some salt and a squeeze of lemon. This recipe elevates them further with the addition of 2 kinds of coriander (the spice and the leaf, also known as cilantro).

1 lb. (450g) green beans, trimmed

2 tbsp (30ml) extra-virgin olive oil

3 garlic cloves, thinly sliced

1 tbsp (5g) crushed coriander seed (see note)

Kosher salt and fresh cracked pepper to taste

Fresh cilantro and lime wedges for garnish

Serves 2–4 people.

Instructions

1. Boil green beans in a pot with heavily salted water for 3–5 minutes until cooked but still crunchy and vibrant green.

2. While beans cook, warm up extra-virgin olive oil in a frying pan on medium-high heat. Add crushed coriander seeds and garlic slices. Sizzle for 2–3 minutes to infuse flavors.

3. Add cooked green beans to the frying pan. Toss with coriander and garlic mixture and continue to fry for 2–3 minutes. Taste and adjust seasoning if needed.

4. Transfer green beans to a serving bowl, garnish with fresh cilantro leaves, and serve with a wedge of lime.

Notes: For optimal coriander flavor, crush seeds with a mortar and pestle. Although I prefer serving this side dish warm, it will also work at room temperature.

Grilled Eggplant with Garlic Yogurt

Eggplants have a bad reputation. They can be bitter, mushy, bland, or just plain unappetizing if not prepared the right way. Grilling eggplants accentuates their meaty texture, which I personally love. This recipe can be scaled up or down. The same method can be applied to zucchini.

3–4 long Asian eggplants

Extra-virgin olive oil for brushing

Kosher salt

¾ cup (190g) plain yogurt (or substitute coconut yogurt)

1–2 garlic cloves, minced

1 tsp (5ml) lemon juice

2 tbsp (2.5g) fresh dill, finely chopped

2 tbsp (2.5g) fresh mint, finely chopped

Kosher salt and fresh cracked pepper to taste

Chili flakes, sumac, dill fronds, and/or mint leaves for garnish

Serves 2–4 people.

Instructions

1. Prepare eggplants by slicing them in half vertically. Using a small paring knife, cut a ¼" (6mm) deep crosshatch pattern into the flesh of the eggplants. Rub the cut parts with a small amount of extra-virgin olive oil and sprinkle lightly with salt.

2. Grill eggplants for 5–8 minutes, until fork-tender and charred slightly. Transfer to a plate.

3. While the eggplants cool slightly, prepare the yogurt sauce. Combine yogurt, minced garlic, lemon juice, chopped dill, and mint. Season with salt and pepper to taste. The yogurt sauce should be slightly runny, so feel free to add some olive oil or water to help thin it out.

4. Dollop yogurt on a serving plate and arrange eggplants on top. Garnish with chili flakes, sumac, dill fronds, and mint leaves. Enjoy while eggplants are still warm and yogurt sauce is still cool.

Notes: This recipe should be prepared just before serving. Yogurt sauce can be made ahead and stored in the fridge for 1 day.

Sweet and Sour Roasted Carrots

This recipe hits all the notes: sweet, spicy, sour, and herbaceous, making it a perfect side to accompany any main dish.

1–2 bunches of young carrots, tops trimmed

2 tbsp (30ml) extra-virgin olive oil

2 tbsp (30ml) maple syrup

1 tsp (5g) smoked paprika

1 tsp (5g) garlic powder

1 tsp (2g) ground coriander

Kosher salt and fresh cracked pepper to taste

Crushed toasted pistachios and chimichurri (recipe on page 194) for garnish

Serves 2–4 people.

Instructions

1. Preheat your oven to 375°F (190°C).

2. On a parchment-lined baking sheet, arrange carrots in a single layer.

3. In a small bowl, whisk together extra-virgin olive oil, maple syrup, smoked paprika, garlic powder, coriander, a big pinch of kosher salt, and a few grinds of black pepper.

4. Drizzle the carrots with the olive oil and maple mixture and toss. Bake for 30–40 minutes, or until carrots are tender. Keep a watchful eye as the maple syrup can scorch.

5. Once ready, transfer the carrots to a serving plate, garnish with toasted pistachios, and serve with chimichurri on the side.

Notes: This recipe can be prepared with larger carrots, cut into 2" (5cm) chunks on the bias.

Roasted Cauliflower with Tahini and Salsa Macha

Here's another recipe adapted from my mother's repertoire of Middle Eastern dishes. Fried cauliflower with lemon juice brings back so many memories; it's one of those side dishes that appeared frequently on our dinner table. In recent years, my mother switched to oven-roasting cauliflower for a healthier and less greasy alternative. I'm adapting her recipe with a couple of sauces that I think give the cauliflower a little more oomph and texture.

1 head of cauliflower, separated into florets

2 tbsp (30ml) olive oil

1 tsp (5g) garlic powder

1 tsp (2g) ground coriander

1 tsp kosher salt

Tahini Sauce

2 tbsp (30ml) tahini

1 tbsp (15ml) lemon juice

Cold water

Kosher salt and fresh ground pepper to taste

Optional Garnishes

Salsa Macha (recipe on page 195)

Lemon wedges

Chopped cilantro leaves

Serves 4–6 people.

Instructions

1. Preheat your oven to 400°F (200°C).

2. In a large bowl, toss the cauliflower florets with olive oil, garlic powder, ground coriander, and salt. Transfer to a lined baking sheet and bake for 30–40 minutes. Test for doneness by inserting a knife through a cauliflower stem. If the knife slides in easily, the cauliflower is ready.

3. While the cauliflower roasts, prepare the tahini sauce. In a small bowl, whisk together the tahini and lemon juice. This will cause the tahini to thicken. Add a tablespoon or two of cold water and continue to whisk until you reach a runny consistency. Season with salt and pepper to taste.

4. Transfer the roasted cauliflower to a serving dish. Drizzle with tahini sauce and salsa macha. Garnish with chopped cilantro leaves and serve with lemon wedges.

Notes: Leftover roasted cauliflower can be stored in an airtight container in the refrigerator for up to 2 days. This dish can be served hot out of the oven or at room temperature.

Charred Bok Choy

Though steamed or stir-fried bok choy tends to dominate, I enjoy grilling it as well. This recipe is certainly adaptable, and you can opt to pan-fry or steam the bok choy instead if you prefer. The sauce is a soy-based, Chinese-inspired combination of salty, sweet, spicy, and sour flavors. This recipe can also be prepared with other hearty greens like Joi Choi, sprouting broccoli, or rapini.

5–6 baby bok choy, sliced in half vertically

1 tbsp (15ml) vegetable oil

Pinch of kosher salt

2 tbsp (30ml) low sodium soy sauce

2 tbsp (30ml) rice wine vinegar

1 garlic clove, finely minced

1 tbsp (7g) ginger, finely minced

1 tbsp (15ml) sesame oil

1 tsp (5g) sugar

1 tsp (5ml) hot sauce (optional)

Kosher salt and fresh cracked pepper to taste

Cilantro leaves and toasted sesame seeds for garnish

Serves 2–4 people.

Instructions

1. This step is optional, but recommended. Blanch the bok choy halves in boiling water for 30–60 seconds, then transfer to a plate.

2. Rub bok choy with vegetable oil and season lightly with kosher salt.

3. Grill on medium-high heat in a griddle pan or on a barbecue until charred and slightly softened (5–8 minutes). Do not overcook; the bok choy should still have some bite to it. Transfer to a serving dish.

4. In a small bowl or jar, combine the soy sauce, rice wine vinegar, garlic, ginger, sesame oil, sugar, and hot sauce if using. Stir well to combine. This mixture should be well balanced, but if needed, season with kosher salt and pepper to taste.

5. Drizzle the dressing on the grilled bok choi. Garnish with fresh cilantro leaves and sesame seeds.

Condiments

Hand-Chopped Chimichurri

Chimichurri is an herbaceous condiment from Argentina, now popular around the world. It is traditionally served alongside grilled proteins but also works wonderfully with grilled zucchini, eggplant, and cauliflower steaks. What I love about this recipe is that it comes together very quickly. When garden parsley is growing wild, I make chimichurri. There is absolutely no proof to substantiate this, but it is a fun story nonetheless: Some argue that the word chimichurri came about from a corruption of English words such as "Jimmy's Curry" or "Jimmy McCurry." One story specifically cites Jimmy, an Englishman who fought alongside Argentinians for independence. As his name was difficult to pronounce, it morphed into chimichurri. Tell this story at your next barbecue and see who falls for it.

½ cup (50g) packed flat-leaf parsley

3 garlic cloves, peeled

1–2 hot peppers

1 tbsp (3g) dried oregano or 2 tbsp (6g) fresh oregano

½ cup (120ml) extra-virgin olive oil

3 tbsp (45ml) red wine vinegar

Kosher salt and fresh cracked pepper to taste

Instructions

1. Chop the parsley, garlic, and peppers as finely or as coarsely as you desire and add to a bowl.

2. Add the dried oregano or chopped fresh oregano.

3. Add the olive oil and vinegar.

4. Stir well and season with salt and pepper. Transfer to a mason jar or glass bottle.

5. Use it right away, or as another alternative, let the flavors meld in the refrigerator for a day before using. Oil may solidify in the fridge. Let the jar or bottle rest on the counter for an hour before using so that the oil can liquify, if necessary.

Notes: Do not use curly parsley for this recipe. Store the chimichurri in an airtight container in the refrigerator for up to a week. I prefer hand-chopping as it gives me more control and doesn't bruise the parsley; however, in a pinch, you can use a food processor. Omit the hot pepper entirely for a mild version.

Salsa Macha

This umami-packed recipe is a great way to repurpose dried chiles. Use this salsa on fried eggs, grilled proteins, tacos, and fried tofu. Treat it like a seasoning bomb and use it whenever you're looking for that hit of flavor.

1 cup (240ml) light olive oil or vegetable oil

3 tbsp (25g) peanuts

2 garlic cloves, peeled

1.5 oz (42g) dried Mexican chiles (guajillo, pasilla, arbol, or a mix) torn into pieces, with most of the seeds removed and discarded (about ½–1 cup)

1 tbsp (9g) untoasted sesame seeds

2 tbsp (30ml) red wine vinegar

2 tsp (8g) white sugar

1 tsp (1g) dried oregano

Kosher salt and fresh cracked pepper to taste

Instructions

1. In a stainless steel or nonreactive pan or skillet, add your olive oil, torn chiles, peanuts, garlic, and sesame seeds. Cook on medium heat, stirring occasionally until garlic and sesame seeds have browned slightly. This could take anywhere between 3 and 5 minutes. Keep an eye out—we don't want our mix burning, but rather toasting lightly in the oil.

2. Allow the mix to cool for 15 minutes. Add vinegar, sugar, oregano, and salt. Stir to combine. Set aside.

3. Make sure the mix has cooled completely, then transfer to a blender or food processor and blitz to desired consistency. I like it a little chunky and crunchy.

4. Transfer to an airtight mason jar and refrigerate.

Notes: Because of the relatively small amount of vinegar, this salsa will keep in the refrigerator for up to 4 weeks. Scale back the recipe by half for a smaller batch. Oil may solidify during refrigeration. Let it sit on the counter for 1 hour before serving to allow the oil to liquify. Almonds may be used instead of peanuts.

Ají

My partner makes this tangy vinegar-based condiment almost weekly. It goes perfectly with fried eggs, empanadas, and roasted potatoes.

1–2 hot peppers, finely chopped

¼ cup (45g) tomato, finely chopped

4 green onions, finely chopped

¼ cup (4g) cilantro, finely chopped

¼ cup (60ml) white vinegar

2 tbsp (30ml) extra-virgin olive oil

1 tbsp (15ml) lime juice

Kosher salt and fresh cracked pepper to taste

Instructions

Combine all ingredients in a mason jar or nonreactive mixing bowl. Allow the mix to rest for at least 1 hour so flavors can infuse. Taste and adjust seasoning.

Notes: Ají will keep in the fridge for 5 days, although it will lose some of its vibrancy and color. You can refresh it by adding some chopped fresh cilantro and green onions.

Shattah

A spicy, slightly oily condiment, shattah goes well with an array of dishes. Add it to labneh, hummus, tacos, or stews. The salting technique in this recipe can be applied to a range of peppers. It helps draw out moisture from the peppers while seasoning them in the process. I also love making red shattah using Fresno peppers.

1 cup (100g) jalapeño peppers, trimmed and roughly chopped

1 tsp (5g) kosher salt

2 tbsp (30ml) white distilled vinegar

Olive oil

Instructions

1. Add the chopped jalapeños and salt to a mason jar or bowl. Stir to combine, cover, and refrigerate for 1 day. This should help draw out some of the excess water present in the jalapeños.

2. The next day, using a sieve, strain the jalapeño mixture. Transfer drained jalapeño pieces to a food processor, add vinegar, and pulse to desired consistency. You can keep it a little chunky (preferred) or puree it. It's up to you.

3. Transfer the mixture to a clean mason jar or other glass container, cover it with a layer of olive oil, and refrigerate.

Notes: This condiment will keep for up to 1 month in the fridge. The oil may solidify. Take the jar out of the fridge an hour before you need to use it so the oil can liquify. Although I prefer making this with jalapeños (as they are not overly spicy), you can also use serrano peppers, or if you are truly bold, Thai green peppers. Swap out some of the hot peppers and replace them with bell peppers for a milder version.

Preservation

Pickling and Fermenting

For me, there is no greater joy than transforming homegrown produce into preserves that further extend their shelf life. Pickling and fermenting, both preservation techniques that involve submerging vegetables and spices in a solution, are similar and yet very different.

Pickling refers to the process of preserving fruits and vegetables in a vinegar solution. Examples include dill pickles, pickled ginger, and dilly beans. Although pickling lends itself to water bath canning (shelf-stable preservation), I will be focusing on refrigerator pickles in this book (pickles that must be refrigerated). Shelf-stable canning techniques and recommendations vary from region to region, and I encourage you to consult your local health authorities for up-to-date information.

Fermentation, or more precisely lacto-fermentation, involves submerging vegetables and fruits in a brine solution (salt and water). Rather than killing bacteria (like pickling typically does), this process takes a different approach. The world is full of bad bacteria (e.g., Clostridium botulinum) and good bacteria (e.g., Lactobacillus). When done correctly, fermentation kills or suppresses the bad bacteria while giving the good bacteria a chance to thrive. This process transforms the vegetables and/or fruits into healthy, probiotic-rich foods.

So how does this transformation take place? There are 2 stages to this process.

In stage one, vegetables and/or fruits are submerged in a brine solution that is salty enough to suppress or kill harmful bacteria. During this stage, good bacteria survive. In stage two, Lactobacillus organisms begin converting lactose and other sugars present in the food into lactic acid. This creates an acidic environment. If you've ever tasted kimchee or sauerkraut, you'll notice they have an acidity to them that is different from a traditional pickle. They taste tangy as opposed to pickled. Furthermore, they may even tingle on your tongue. This fizziness is attributed to the carbon dioxide that is generated in the fermentation process.

For a successful fermentation project, you will need to ensure that:

- The brine solution is just right
- Your equipment is clean (preferably sterile)
- You use a special fermentation lid

Too much salt in your brine solution and you risk killing both good and bad bacteria. Too little salt and you may not fully suppress the bad bacteria. Generally, the recommended brine solution should be in the 2%–5% range. This translates to 2g–5g of salt for every 100g of water. I recommend using kosher salt, pickling salt, or sea salt. Filtered or spring water is preferred over tap water because the chlorine in tap water could affect fermentation. I recommend using a kitchen scale to achieve the desired salt:water ratio. Alternatively, a good place to start is 2 tbsp of salt to 4 cups of water (which works out to 34g of salt to 946g of water – a 3.5% ratio).

A specialized fermentation lid and weights will help keep the food submerged in the solution while ensuring that carbon dioxide can escape. Do you need to use a specialized fermentation lid? No. You can certainly use a standard lid and burp your jars daily by cracking them open to let the gases escape. That being said, a specialized lid will be safer and more convenient.

During the fermentation process, a white substance may form in your jar. This is called Kahm yeast. It is a strain of wild yeast that forms a white layer and covers the top of your ferment. It is not harmful. Simply skim it off and continue. Generally speaking, you will not encounter this issue with my recipes as the recommended fermentation times will be a few days. If mold appears (any fuzzy green, yellow, black, red, or pink growths), I recommend discarding the batch and starting over. The old adage applies: "When in doubt, throw it out."

There are books and resources dedicated to fermentation, and I would certainly recommend referring to them if this is something you want to explore in greater detail. The recipes I provide in this book are meant for you to test the waters. They are simple, and if followed correctly, relatively foolproof.

Refrigerator Pickle, 7 Ways

Pickling is a great way to not only preserve your harvest, but transform it into something completely different. From pickled red onions to escabeche, I hope this recipe inspires you to come up with your own flavor combinations. Note that this recipe is not meant for water bath canning. The final product must be refrigerated.

Basic Pickling Solution

1 cup (240ml) white distilled vinegar

1 cup (240ml) water

1 tbsp (15g) kosher, pickling, or sea salt

1 tsp (4g) white sugar

Instructions

1. Make the pickling solution: In a nonreactive pot, add 1 cup water, 1 cup white vinegar, 1 tbsp salt, and 1 tsp sugar (scale up your recipe if you're making a large batch). Warm the solution on medium heat and stir to dissolve the salt and sugar. This should take around 2–4 minutes. Once dissolved, turn off the heat and allow solution to cool completely.

2. To sterilized mason jars, add your desired flavorings and chopped vegetables.

3. Cover with the cooled vinegar solution, tap to release air bubbles, seal, and refrigerate.

4. Refrigerator pickles should be ready within 48 hours, but I find they taste best after a week.

Notes: Refrigerator pickles will last in the refrigerator for several months, although their flavor and crispness begin to deteriorate after 2 months. Some of my favorites are:

- Sliced red onion, garlic, black peppercorns, anise
- Escabeche (carrots, onions, jalapeños, garlic, black pepper, coriander seeds)
- Dill pickle (cucumber spears or slices, dill, garlic, mustard seeds, black peppercorns)
- Sliced radish, peppercorns
- Dilly beans (green beans, dill, garlic, black peppercorns, hot peppers)
- Sweet peppers
- Boiled beets

Fermented Hot Sauce

A summertime favorite, fermented hot sauce is easy to make and adds a spicy kick to tacos, soups, stews, and more. It's also an excellent way to preserve peppers long-term in the fridge. Please read the fermentation primer on the previous pages before proceeding with this recipe.

2 cups (480ml) filtered or spring water

1 tbsp (17g) kosher, pickling, or sea salt

Combination of red, yellow, and orange peppers (hot and sweet)

1 garlic clove, peeled

½ medium white onion, peeled

1 tbsp (15ml) white distilled vinegar

Makes 1 pint (500ml) jar. Scale up as needed, however, make sure that you maintain the same brine ratio.

Instructions

1. In a nonreactive pot, combine 2 cups of water with 1 tbsp of kosher salt, pickling salt, or sea salt. Warm to dissolve the salt and then set aside to cool.

2. While the brine cools, prepare the peppers. Cut your peppers into rings or chunks. Size doesn't matter since we will eventually blend them (see notes).

3. Add one clove of garlic and the white onion to the bottom of a mason jar. Carefully pack peppers into the jar, pressing down firmly as you fill it. Apply fermenting weight, if using.

4. When the brine has cooled, pour it into the mason jar and cover the peppers. Tap the jar a few times to release any air bubbles. Discard any leftover brine. Apply fermenting lid and follow the manufacturer's instructions.

5. Ferment on the counter for 3–5 days. The longer you ferment, the tangier the sauce will be. The brine may get cloudy, and that's completely normal. If you see any unusual growths, discard the batch (refer to fermentation primer for more information).

6. Strain the contents of the mason jar, reserving the brine. Add peppers, onions, and garlic to a blender with a splash of the brine. Blend on high until homogenous (1–2 minutes). Add 1 tbsp of white vinegar and blend again for 30 seconds. Taste and adjust seasoning. If the sauce is too thick, add more brine and blend again on high speed for 30 seconds.

7. Transfer to a clean hot sauce bottle or mason jar and refrigerate for up to 6 months.

Notes: Use gloves when handling hot peppers. Select peppers with similar or complementary colors. Yellow, orange, and red peppers blend nicely together. Do not mix them with green or purple peppers or you'll end up with an unappetizingly brown hot sauce. If you like your hot sauce to be extremely potent, use hot peppers only. If you prefer your hot sauce on the milder side, combine hot peppers with sweet peppers. The salt/water ratio is critical. Make sure to follow the recipe as outlined.

Harvest Giardiniera

This recipe for Italian-style giardiniera can be changed up to suit your taste; it is, however, important to maintain the correct brine ratio to ensure safety.

4 cups (960ml) filtered or spring water

2 tbsp (30g) kosher, pickling, or sea salt

Mixed vegetables (carrots, celery, cauliflower, peppers, onions) cut into bite-sized pieces

2 garlic cloves, peeled

2 bay leaves

1 tsp (3g) yellow mustard seeds

1 tsp (3g) black peppercorns

1 tsp (3g) fennel seeds

2 tbsp (30ml) white distilled vinegar (optional)

Makes 1 quart (1L).

Instructions

1. In a nonreactive pot, combine 4 cups of water with 2 tbsp of kosher salt, pickling salt, or sea salt. Warm to dissolve the salt and then set aside to cool.

2. Place the mixed vegetables, garlic, bay leaves, yellow mustard seeds, black peppercorns, and fennel seeds in a mason jar and pack down tightly. Apply fermenting weight, if using.

3. When the brine has cooled, pour it into the mason jar and cover the vegetables. Discard any leftover brine. Tap the jar a few times to release any air bubbles. Apply fermenting lid and follow the manufacturer's instructions.

4. Ferment on the counter for 3–5 days. The longer you ferment, the tangier the vegetables will be. The brine may get cloudy, and that's completely normal. If you see any unusual growths, discard the batch (refer to fermentation primer for more information).

5. When ready, transfer the jar to the fridge. At this point you can replace the fermentation lid with a standard lid as the cold temperature of the fridge will slow the fermentation process down to a crawl.

6. Optionally, you can add 2 tbsp of white vinegar to help improve the flavor.

Notes: Although fermented vegetables will keep for a long time if stored properly, I recommend you keep them for no longer than 1 month in the refrigerator. This is why I prefer to make small batches.

Confit

An ancient technique, confit refers to cooking a protein in fat, generally its own. The thick layer of fat then preserves the protein for a period of time. Thankfully, we live in modern times and have access to luxuries our ancestors probably never imagined (e.g., refrigerators). The term confit can also be applied to preparations of fruits and vegetables, although the method is not necessarily used for the purpose of long-term preservation. The technique is adapted and fat is used to transform foods into something completely different and delicious.

Garlic Confit

Although this recipe features whole garlic cloves, the method can be applied to cherry tomatoes, shallots, leeks, and much more.

2 cups (250g) garlic cloves, peeled

1 cup (240ml) olive oil (see note)

2–3 sprigs of thyme

2–3 sprigs of rosemary

1 tbsp (9g) black peppercorns

Instructions

1. Preheat your oven to 275ºF (135ºC).

2. Place all ingredients in a shallow baking dish. Oil should completely submerge the garlic and aromatics. Depending on the vessel, you may need more or less oil. Cover with a lid or foil and place in a preheated oven.

3. After 30 minutes, check to make sure that the garlic isn't burning. Continue to slow roast for another 25–40 minutes. The end result should be lightly browned garlic cloves that can be crushed easily with the back of a fork.

4. Once cooled, transfer the garlic and oil to a mason jar. Store in the fridge.

Notes: You do not need to use expensive olive oil for this recipe. Garlic confit will store in the fridge for up to one week. Oil may solidify in the fridge. Let the jar sit on your counter for 1 hour before using it so the oil can liquefy again. The fragrant oil can be used in vinaigrettes and other recipes. You may want to consider freezing small portions of garlic confit and oil in small mason jars or freezer bags to use as needed.

Drying the Harvest

From garden to pantry, when your garden is producing an abundance of culinary and medicinal herbs and flowers, the logical next step is to preserve the bounty.

Bundling and hanging: This is one of my favorite ways to dry woody herbs as well as flowers like lavender. It is a tried-and-true method people have been using for centuries. Make bundles of herbs and tie the stems tightly with garden or butcher's twine, leaving about 1 foot (30cm) of extra twine to use for hanging and tying. Once bundled, hang them in a room where humidity is low to avoid spoilage. This method takes time but yields the best results as the herbs dry slowly. Shrinkage is minimized, and the color is preserved. This method works well for drying flowers (including when harvesting seed) and thin-skinned peppers like cayenne and Thai chilis. Thick-skinned peppers should be dried in an oven or dehydrator.

Drying on a screen: Another effective way to dry your herbs and flowers is by placing them on a screen in a warm and bright room. Window screen material is perfect for this as it allows good airflow and reduces the chance of spoilage from moisture. You can purchase window screen material from your local hardware store and make a DIY frame from scrap lumber. I prefer to use one of the window screen inserts from my house. I remove the screen insert and lay it on top of a tall shelving unit. Just like bundling and hanging, this method does take time, but the results are worth the wait.

Using a dehydrator: A dehydrator is a great appliance; in my opinion, it is a must for any serious gardener and grower. They are great for dehydrating fruits, vegetables, flowers, and of course herbs. What I love about them is that they are adjustable in terms of temperature and time, which gives the user a lot of control and accuracy. Tender herbs like basil and parsley may require a lower temperature setting, while woodier herbs like rosemary and sage might need a higher temperature setting. Consult the user manual for specific instructions and recommended settings.

Using an oven: This is my least favorite way to dry herbs and flowers because it is so unpredictable. In fact, if your oven doesn't go as low as 150–175°F (65–80°C), I would recommend you don't use this method. You may end up cooking your herbs, and they will become brown and unappetizing. If your oven does go that low, the technique is quite simple. Set your oven to the lowest possible setting. On a large baking sheet lined with parchment paper, place your cleaned herbs. Try not to overlap them too much since you want them to dry evenly. With this method, you must keep an eye on your oven and check back regularly. You may even have to flip and turn your herbs if you find that they are not drying as evenly as needed. You may also want to consider propping the oven door open with a wooden spoon so that the oven chamber doesn't get too hot. I would stress that if you have the space for it, it's a good idea to invest in a dehydrator that fits your budget and space requirements.

Using a microwave: I'm generally not a fan of using microwaves, but this hack is certainly worthwhile. For a quick fix, you can place herbs in a single layer on a piece of paper towel and microwave for 30 seconds on high. Toss the herbs around, then microwave again in increments of 15 seconds, tossing the herbs at each interval. The result should be crispy and crunchy. In a pinch, the microwave will do, but I still recommend the hanging method to preserve the color and vibrancy of the herb.

Before storing your dried herbs, they must be completely dry and brittle. If there is any moisture left in the leaves, the finished product will spoil. Strip the leaves off the stems and store them in airtight containers or mason jars.

A note on washing: Although the field is split on whether or not to wash herbs before setting them to dry, I recommend washing your edible herbs, spinning them dry in a salad spinner, and laying them on a clean kitchen towel to air dry for an hour before proceeding with the drying options listed above.

Herb Blends

You've dried all these herbs. Now what? There's nothing wrong with storing them in individually labeled containers in your pantry, but why not combine them into classic seasonings you'll use again and again? Consider improvising and creating your own signature blends—get creative! Here are three of my favorite blends. You can prepare them according to the recipes or use them as inspiration to make your own.

All-Purpose Mediterranean Herb Mix

1 part dried oregano

1 part dried thyme

1 part dried rosemary

1 part crushed dried sage

1 part hot pepper flakes (optional)

Herbes de Provence

2 parts dried thyme

2 parts dried rosemary

2 parts dried savory

2 parts dried oregano

1 part lavender flowers (optional)

Za'atar Spice Blend

1 part Syrian thyme (*Origanum syriacum* for authenticity, but you can substitute Greek oregano)

1 part marjoram

1 part sumac

1 part toasted sesame seeds

Herb-Infused Salt

A rather fun and satisfying way to preserve your herb harvest is to make your own herb-infused salts. Not only is this a wonderful preservation technique, infused salts are a great homemade gift. They can be used to season vegetables, proteins, salad dressings, and more. The ratio of salt to flavorings should be 4 to 1. Don't worry too much about being precise since there's wiggle room with the quantities. Ensuring the infused salt is completely dry before storing is essential.

1 cup (280g) coarse sea salt

¼ cup fresh herbs and other flavorings

(see flavor combination suggestions below)

Instructions

1. In a food processor, add your herbs and flavorings. Process until herbs and flavorings are combined and finely chopped.

2. Add coarse salt to the food processor. Process until salt, herbs, and flavorings are combined.

3. Transfer the mixture to a rimmed baking sheet lined with parchment paper and spread evenly. Bake at 225°F (110°C) for 30 minutes to 1 hour. The mixture should be completely dry.

4. Once fully cooled, break up any large chunks and transfer the infused salt to mason jars.

Flavor combinations to try:
- Rosemary and lemon zest
- Cilantro and lime zest
- Thyme and dried garlic

Notes: The herbs need to be completely dry before storing. Keep them in the pantry and use within 6 months. The same process can be applied to sugar. Try infusing sugar with mint, lavender, or lemon verbena.

Freezing the Harvest

Freezing is an easy and accessible way to preserve your harvest to use throughout the winter months. If handled correctly, frozen fruits and vegetables can brighten up any dreary winter day. A few tips to make this as seamless as possible:

- Produce should be washed and thoroughly dried before freezing.
- Consider pre-freezing smaller produce like berries and cherry tomatoes on a tray first and then transferring to freezer bags or containers. This reduces the likelihood of clumping.
- Certain crops benefit from blanching before freezing. These include leafy greens such as kale, chard, and spinach. Green beans can also be blanched for 30 seconds before freezing.
- Certain crops will require processing before freezing. For example, zucchini should be shredded and squeezed to remove as much liquid as possible before freezing. Eggplant can be roasted and pureed before freezing.
- Hot peppers will lose some of their heat in the freezer.
- Remove as much of the air as possible from your freezer bag or container. Not only does this save space, but it will also reduce the chance of freezer burn. A vacuum sealer is a good investment.
- Herbs can be submerged in olive oil or water and frozen in ice cube trays. These flavor-packed cubes can be used at a later time to make pesto, marinades, or salad dressings.
- Try to use your frozen produce within 6–12 months. Any longer and the flavor and/or texture may be compromised.

Compound Butter

Flavored or scented butter is a great way to preserve herbs, edible flowers, and other garden goodness. What I love about making compound butter is that the flavor combinations are endless and the finished product freezes extremely well.

½ lb. (2 sticks or 226g) salted or unsalted butter

3–4 tbsp (4g–5g) herb or flavoring of choice

Instructions

1. In a bowl, combine softened butter and flavoring of choice. Mix well. Alternatively, you can use a small food processor.

2. Serve as is or refrigerate for up to 1 week.

3. Optional freezing method: Transfer the mixture to a sheet of plastic wrap. Carefully form the mixture into a cylinder, using the plastic wrap to help guide you. Roll the cylinder while holding the edges in place to create a tight package, much like a candy wrapper. Cool in the fridge for at least 1 hour. Portion the cylinder into discs and freeze in a container or freezer bag.

Note: For savory compound butter, use salted butter. For sweet compound butter, use unsalted.

Flavor combinations to try:

- Garlic confit and crushed black pepper compound butter to swirl in soup
- Parsley, mint, and chive compound butter to garnish roast potatoes or steamed green beans
- Lavender, lemon zest, and sugar to enjoy with scones and muffins
- Garlic scape compound butter to top roasted or grilled vegetables (made with garlic flower stalks)
- Chili flake compound butter for when you need a spicy kick

Chapter 4

Garden Planning

A successful garden is a well-planned and well-thought-out garden. In my early gardening days, I was somewhat of an experimenter. I needed to get my hands on all the seeds and seedlings, regardless of whether or not they were suitable for my climate, space, or skill set.

While experimenting can be fun, it can also lead to tremendous disappointments. One example I refer to often when discussing the importance of planning is that of a client in Toronto, Canada. She decided to grow luffa gourd in her small townhouse backyard. She had seen many gardeners grow it successfully on social media, some even doing so in containers, and felt like she wanted to be part of the luffa growing movement. Her luffa vine grew uncontrollably, suffocating nearby crops and producing one single gourd which didn't get a chance to mature on the vine long enough before the first frost. It was an utterly disastrous, unproductive season for her. I had advised her against growing luffa, however, the social media pull and FOMO (Fear Of Missing Out) clouded her judgment.

I am all for experimenting in the garden and trying new crops and varieties, as long as they have a good chance of success. How can you help mitigate the risk of failure, grow abundantly, and still enjoy the process? For me, it boils down to understanding and appreciating your climate, space, level of personal commitment, and limitations.

- Understand your climate and growing zone. Do you know your zone number? Do you live in a microclimate? Have you tracked your first and last frost dates, if applicable?
- Understand your space limitations. How big is your garden? Do you only have room for containers?
- Understand your limitations: How much time can you devote to your garden? Are you a hands-on gardener? Do you plan to travel throughout the growing season and be away from your garden?

Being honest with yourself, using your space wisely, and understanding what will and will not work in your region will set you on the right path toward success.

Hardiness Zones and Microclimates

The USDA (United States Department of Agriculture) has divided the United States into hardiness zones (also referred to by some as growing zones). These numbered zones include regions with similar minimum average annual temperatures. The lower the zone number is, the lower the winter temperatures in that zone. Each zone is on average 10°F warmer or colder than the adjacent zone. Zones can be further divided into sub-zones. For example, zone 6a and 6b are adjacent zones with a 5°F differential in average annual extreme minimum temperature.

Europe, Canada, and Australia have similar systems. The Canadian hardiness map can often be confusing for home gardeners because it uses a different system than the map employed in the US. As an example, this means that the same parts of Toronto, Canada, can be considered zone 6 by USDA standards or zone 5 by Canadian standards. The issue with relying on your zone number alone to make planning and planting decisions is that you are not getting a complete picture of the growing conditions and climate in your space.

The purpose of a hardiness map (or zones) is to help gardeners determine whether a perennial will survive and thrive in a certain area. Perennials are plants that will continue to grow year after year in zones where they are listed as hardy. For example, in zone 6, thyme, oregano, blueberries, roses, hydrangeas, and many other edible and ornamental plants are considered perennial. In a garden center or nursery, these plants are typically grouped and will almost always bear a tag that labels them as perennial. Tags may also include the number of the zone where they are considered hardy. The good news is that your local garden center or nursery should only carry perennial plants that are hardy to your zone.

Avocados are hardy in zones 8–11. This means that someone in zone 6 would probably not be able to buy an avocado tree at their local nursery. Lemon trees are best suited for zones 9–11; however, they can be grown in containers in cooler zones if sheltered properly indoors or in a heated greenhouse during the winter months. For that reason, someone in zone 6 might be able to purchase a lemon tree, with the understanding that it should not be grown outdoors in the ground.

A plant's hardiness is also related to the length of the local growing season and can apply to annual crops as well. For example, the growing season is on average 180 days long in zone 6, whereas it's 265 days long in zone 9. This includes both cooler spring and fall days as well as warm summer days. Going back to the luffa gourd example, someone in zone 6 would have to think hard about whether or not they should consider growing it as it can take 100+ days to mature—that's 100+ days of warm summer weather.

There's quite a bit of nuance to this concept. Hardiness zones should only be used as a general guideline because in reality, microclimates are real and measurable phenomena that can affect minimum temperatures greatly, especially in urban centers. A garden that's surrounded by tall skyscrapers will experience different temperatures and conditions than one in an open field. A raised bed garden that is insulated and protected from snow will experience different conditions than an east-facing twentieth-floor balcony garden. Understanding your specific conditions from year to year will give you the best insights, preparing you for the planning process.

Leveraging Your Space Efficiently

After determining if a plant will grow and thrive in your climate, you'll need to assess whether or not you can devote the square footage to it that it needs to thrive. Certain vining crops can take over your entire backyard if you let them, snuffing out everything else in their wake. Luffa gourd vines can grow up to 30' (9m) long, making them extremely difficult to manage in small spaces. For this reason, I do not grow pumpkin or vining squash like butternut in my small urban backyard. The space/yield ratio is just not favorable. Although they can be grown vertically (refer to Chapter 5), I would rather grow high-yield crops that do not take up a large footprint in my small backyard. However, I will certainly grow pumpkins and squash at my allotment plot or on larger pieces of land to which I have access from year to year.

For a new gardener, it's difficult to visualize the space requirements of a crop by simply looking at a seed packet or by holding a small seedling full of potential. That 5" (13cm) pumpkin seedling will grow into a 12' (3.6m) vine under favorable conditions. That corn seed will germinate and could grow into a 6' (1.8m) stalk. That cabbage seedling can grow into a 3' (90cm) wide plant. Understanding and appreciating how large a crop may get at maturity is the best way to decide if it's worth growing in your limited space.

If you only have access to a balcony, there are some additional considerations. Is your balcony open from above, or does it have a ceiling? If so, you must consider plant heights at maturity. Growing pole beans, for example, might not be a good idea as they could easily reach the ceiling; choose bush beans instead. Focusing on high-yield, small-footprint crops with shorter growth habits is recommended. They will be easier to manage and water, and they'll allow you to still enjoy your balcony without it turning into a tangled mess. The direction of the balcony and the number of hours of sunlight it receives are also critical for success. In the Northern Hemisphere, a south-facing balcony will receive a decent amount of light and can support multiple types of crops. A north-facing balcony will receive very little direct sunlight, making it more difficult to grow some warm-weather crops like tomatoes and peppers.

If you are growing on a paved terrace with unobstructed access to the sun, you do not have to contend with the same limitations as a balcony grower. However, you will only be able to grow in containers. But because most crops are well suited for container and vertical growing, you will have plenty of crop options to choose from (refer to Chapters 2 and 5).

High-yield, small-footprint crops that work well in small gardens include salad greens, Asian greens, peas, bush and pole beans, tomatoes, peppers, cucumbers, and zucchini. One way to maximize the use of space is to employ succession planting, which is covered in more detail in Chapter 5.

A note on fruit trees: Though this book focuses primarily on vegetables you can grow from seed, I would be remiss if I did not mention the benefits of planting fruit trees in the garden. If you have the space for them and your climate can sustain them, fruit trees (as well as fruit bushes like raspberries and blueberries) can provide you with a bountiful yearly harvest of fruit that you can preserve, enjoy fresh, or give away to friends and family. I personally have a pear tree and a peach tree in my backyard. They are part of my overall garden-to-table strategy and have been producing bushels of fruit for several years. They are certainly worth the investment and should be considered in your garden planning. If this is a topic of interest, I recommend you seek out advice from your local nurseries.

Taking Personal Inventory

We've all been there. Getting swept away in ideas, dreams, and seed catalogs is a winter ritual for many gardeners, myself included. It has taken me several years to understand and appreciate my limitations and requirements and how to consider them when planning my garden. Our needs, time commitments, and financial situations change from year to year, and it is critical to recognize this so that we can grow gardens that will bring us joy, satisfaction, and a sense of accomplishment.

What need is your garden fulfilling?

Is it an emotional need? Are you looking to connect with nature? Or are you simply looking for big bountiful harvests to cook, preserve, and share? Do you really need to grow that luffa gourd?

If you desire a tranquil, relaxing space, consider including flowers and medicinal herbs. If the ability to harvest flowers and make seasonal arrangements for yourself and your friends is a priority to you, consider planting cut flowers in your garden. An edible garden doesn't have to be comprised entirely of edible plants. Crafting a vision for your space will help you not only in the garden planning process but also allow you to figure out what it is you truly want from your garden. Your needs can change from year to year as well; they aren't set in stone. Allow them to guide you in the planning process.

How much time are you willing to put into the garden?

Can you spare at least one hour a day? Or will you only be able to tend to the garden a couple of times a week? Are you going on holiday during the growing season? If your time will be limited, consider growing hands-off crops that require little to no maintenance such as lettuce, beets, carrots, potatoes, herbs, kale, and bush beans. Other than the occasional pest check, these are truly set-it-and-forget-it crops. Be honest with yourself. The last thing I would want is for your garden to feel like a chore.

Are you willing to spend the necessary funds?

Whether we care to admit it or not, gardening can get expensive. Seeds, seed starting equipment, raised beds, soil, amendments, vertical supports, irrigation equipment, and other start-up costs and recurring expenses truly can add up. In many ways, designing and creating a garden is a work of art, a living, breathing work of art that might take several seasons to fully complete. You don't have to build raised beds in your first year. You don't need to invest in an irrigation system right away. You can get your hands on seed packets at local meetups and swaps. Shop for bargains (for example, perennial plants are typically discounted in the fall). The dollar store can be a great place to source garden gadgets and accessories.

The Importance of Flowers in the Edible Garden

An abundant garden is a diverse garden that includes a range of edible and ornamental crops. In addition to providing gorgeous blooms for you to enjoy, flowers can attract pollinators to your garden. Certain crops require pollinators to set fruit, such as cucumbers, squash, and other members of the cucurbit family. Without pollinator activity in your garden, you would have to pollinate these crops by hand, which can be quite cumbersome.

A few tips to consider when adding flowers to your garden design:

- **Blooms all season.** Grow a range of flowers that bloom at different times throughout the season. This not only offers you visual interest but provides nectar to important insect pollinators such as butterflies and bees, as well as hummingbirds.

- **Ideal conditions.** When selecting perennial flowers, make sure that they are planted in a location that suits their needs long-term (i.e., light, soil, and space requirements).

- **Dual purpose.** Certain pollinator-supporting flowers can also be used as cut flowers, further extending their use. Who doesn't love a fresh bouquet of homegrown flowers? Other flowers such as borage are also edible.

- **Prioritize native species.** When selecting pollinator-friendly plants, consider native species (those indigenous to your area) as they can be quite helpful in attracting native bees and other beneficial insects such as parasitic wasps. Consult your local conservation authority to learn more about your local native species.

The following table outlines some of my favorite pollinator-attracting flowers and their various uses.

Flower	Annual/Perennial	Bloom Period	Cut Flower	Edible Flower
Calendula	Annual	Spring to fall	Yes	Yes
Salvia	Perennial Zone 6	Spring	Yes	No *
Marigold	Annual	Spring to fall	Yes	Yes
Lavender	Perennial Zone 6	Summer	Yes	Yes
Nasturtium	Annual	Summer to fall	No	Yes
Borage	Annual	Spring to summer	No	Yes
Yarrow	Perennial Zone 3	Late spring to fall	Yes	Yes
Cosmos	Annual	Summer to fall	Yes	No **
Milkweed	Perennial Zone 4	Spring to summer	No	No
Sunflower	Annual	Summer to fall	Yes	Yes
Zinnia	Annual	Summer to fall	Yes	Yes
Coneflower	Perennial Zone 3	Summer to fall	Yes	Yes

* Ornamental salvias are not edible (although not poisonous). Culinary salvia (sage) is edible.

** Although not poisonous, cosmos flowers are not typically consumed.

Disclaimer: Bloom period will vary depending on zone, variety, and seed starting method. The perennial nature of certain flowers depends not only on the growing zone but also on other possible effects due to microclimates and other factors. Most flowers purchased from garden centers and nurseries are treated and may not be suitable for consumption. When in doubt, do not consume.

Theme Gardens

Garden planning can seem intimidating for the first-time gardener. The options seem limitless. In true garden-to-table fashion, I want you to think about what you or your family love to eat. Do you have a daily green smoothie? Are you into juicing? Do you enjoy Mexican cuisine? Italian cuisine? Are you a tea drinker?

Answering these questions will help you determine which crops to prioritize in your garden. Included below are sample crop combinations that should help get your creative juices flowing:

- **Smoothie or Juice Garden:** Kale, spinach, beetroot, strawberries, cucumbers, Swiss chard, mint.
- **Salsa garden:** Tomatoes, spring onions, onions, hot peppers, bell peppers, cilantro.
- **Pickling garden:** Radish, carrots, cucumbers, green beans, dill.
- **Salad garden:** Lettuce, kale, radish, carrots, tomatoes, cucumbers.
- **Pizza garden:** Tomatoes, basil, oregano, peppers.
- **Tea garden:** Mint, lemon balm, lavender, chamomile.

Chapter 5

Growing Techniques

One of the most life-changing lessons I learned early on in my gardening journey is that growing food cannot and must not be limited to those with big backyards or acres of land. There are millions of people living in apartments, condos, and townhouses in urban centers who deserve to discover the joys of edible gardening and homegrown produce just as much as their suburban and rural counterparts. Helping people grow abundantly in small spaces has been my passion ever since.

For years, I grew food exclusively on balconies and terraces. Granted, my yields were pitiful compared to those of people with access to land. However, that was not the point. In my opinion, it is still better to grow some of your own food than none at all. When I stopped focusing on quantity, my eyes opened to all the possibilities that small space gardening can bring.

This chapter will focus on various techniques and strategies that can be applied by all gardeners, regardless of how much space they have available to them.

Growing in Containers

What constitutes a container? It could be a plastic pot, a half-barrel, a terracotta pot, a grow bag, or a window box. Some of the benefits of growing in containers include:

- **Accessibility.** Growing in containers makes edible gardening accessible and enjoyable for those with limited space, as well as people with limited mobility, including the young and the elderly. Growing in containers is also perfect for renters since no permanent structures are needed.

- **Versatility.** Containers come in all shapes and sizes, allowing you to create a garden space that works for you and your needs.

- **Aesthetics.** With a plethora of possible looks, textures, and colors, containers can add to the overall aesthetics of your space.

- **Minimal weeding.** Due to the limited surface area, weeds are less likely to take hold in a container, making them very easy to maintain.

- **Mobility and flexibility.** Containers can be moved around as plants grow to create more space as needed.

- **Convenience.** By placing your containers close to your patio door or kitchen, you can easily access them as needed.

- **Pest resistance.** You generally don't have to worry about burrowing pests like rats, voles, or mice when growing in containers.

- **Year-round gardening.** Tropical plants grown in containers can be brought inside before winter and continue growing indoors.

I am personally a big fan of container gardening. Even though I have access to land and garden beds, containers allow me to maximize my growing space by expanding out into nontraditional gardening areas of my property such as porches, terraces, roof decks, and windowsills.

A few important considerations about growing in containers:

- Containers tend to dry out quickly, especially on really warm days. They will require more frequent watering than in-ground or raised bed gardens.

- Most containers available for purchase will not have drainage holes. It is imperative to drill drainage holes before using these containers. Failure to do so could lead to a host of problems, including root rot and disease.

- Size matters. Smaller pots (1–3 gallons) are adequate for herbs or shallow-rooted vegetables like lettuce. Medium-sized pots (5–10 gallons) will support peppers and determinate tomatoes. Larger pots (15+ gallons) will allow you to grow large cabbages, multiple peppers, indeterminate tomatoes, or even dahlias. When in doubt, larger is better when it comes to containers. Refer to Chapter 7 for a list of minimum container sizes.

- Plastic pots marketed for gardening purposes will usually be made with food-grade plastic like HDPE (2), LDPE (4), or PP (5). However, it is a good idea to check regardless and make sure the plastic is food safe. This is also referred to as the recycling number (but note that these designations may be different in your local jurisdictions, so please do your due diligence). If you are not comfortable growing in plastic containers, the good news is that there are other natural options available.

Although quite popular, self-watering containers are problematic for several reasons. The water reservoir can be a breeding ground for disease and pests. I do not use these types of containers.

Growing Vertically

When you've exhausted every square inch of available garden space, it's time to look up. By training our vining plants to grow upwards, we can free up precious space on the ground that can be used by non-vining crops. There are many benefits to growing vertically:

- **Less disease pressure.** Elevating the foliage of vining crops helps increase airflow and mitigate the risk of disease.

- **Less pest pressure and fruit loss.** Vertically grown fruits are not readily available to garden pests on the ground. They will also be less susceptible to rot because they are not in contact with moist soil.

- **Ease of maintenance and harvest.** Growing vertically makes it easier to prune and maintain crops. Harvesting is a breeze, and your back will thank you.

Trellises. Flat structures of latticed or crossed bars of wood, metal, or other material used to support climbing plants, Trellises can be placed against a fence, at the end of a raised bed, or even in a rectangular container for crops to climb.

Stakes. Made of bamboo, plastic, or metal and available in varying lengths, stakes are arguably the most widely used plant supports out there. Bamboo stakes are affordable and can last several seasons, whereas plastic-coated metal rods can last a lifetime. They can be used to stake smaller plants like peppers and eggplants as well as taller vining plants like tomatoes. They can also be arranged in a pyramid shape and tied together at the top, creating a perfect A-frame for pole beans and peas to climb.

Arches and arbors. Not only can they support a tremendous amount of vegetation and fruit, but they can also be used as a design element in your garden. They are well suited for climbing roses, clematis, and runner beans. Ranging from DIY cattle panel arches to sophisticated cedar arbors, there are options for all budgets and tastes.

Tomato spirals. As the name suggests, these twisted metal stakes are primarily used to support tomatoes. They are made of durable materials such as stainless or rubber-coated steel. As tomato vines grow, they get twisted around the spiral. This aids in airflow and provides sturdy support for fruit clusters.

Cages. Also referred to as tomato cages, these supports are manufactured with bent and welded metal to create a multi-level round, square, or triangular structure that contains and supports crops. Size matters when it comes to cages. Tomatoes and other vining crops will require tall cages. Smaller cages can be used to support peppers and eggplants.

Growing in Gutters

Another way to grow vertically is by using rain gutters attached to a wall or fence. This allows you to take advantage of growing space that would otherwise be unused. For this DIY project, galvanized steel gutters are my preferred option as they are more suitable for growing food. Neither vinyl nor coated metal gutters have been designed or tested for this application, making galvanized steel a much safer option.

Gutters should be installed on a south-facing, west-facing, or east-facing fence or wall so that they can receive at least six hours of daily sun. In this application, they are essentially a type of container. Therefore, drainage holes must be drilled every 6" (15cm) using a drill bit suitable for metal, such as a cobalt or titanium tipped bit. The gutters need to be capped on each end so that the growing medium does not flow out. They will also need to be level and secured into place with the appropriate connectors and sturdy L brackets.

Depending on weather conditions and location, gutters will require frequent watering because they will certainly dry out quickly. I do not recommend using them in regions with high summer temperatures and regularly occurring heat waves. On really warm days, you may need to water them twice. A drip irrigation system helps take the pressure off. Refer to Chapter 9 for more specific irrigation information.

Due to their size, they will only be suitable for shallow-rooted crops such as baby lettuce, baby greens, radish, strawberries, and bush beans.

Scan the QR code to view a video of my gutter system and the equipment needed to build your own.

Growing in Raised Beds

Growing in raised beds has several advantages:

- If your native soil is of poor quality or too difficult to work with (for example, clay), a raised bed allows you to create a robust and usable growing environment for crops to thrive.
- You have full control over the growing medium and amendments.
- From a comfort and safety perspective, a raised bed is easier to harvest and maintain.
- Soil compaction is minimized or eliminated since there's no need to ever step into a raised bed.
- They can be an integral part of your garden design and aesthetic.

There are several options on the market available for the home gardener, ranging from prefabricated wood beds to stainless steel, zinc, or plastic options. Building your beds from rot-resistant untreated wood (cedar or redwood) is my preferred method because it allows you to build a completely customized setup tailored for your space and needs. A few important considerations when building your own raised beds:

- **Easy Access.** Ensure that your beds can be accessed easily for daily tasks such as planting, weeding, pruning, and harvesting. A good rule of thumb is to build beds that are 4' (1.2m) wide when they are accessible from all sides, or 2' (60cm) wide when accessible from one side only (for example, if the bed is against a fence). 2' (60cm) is a comfortable length for adults to reach without straining or injuring themselves.

- **Height matters.** Ensure that your beds are at least 18" (45 cm) tall. Taller beds are more comfortable to harvest and maintain. They also hold a larger volume of soil, which can be beneficial if the native soil below is of inadequate quality.

- **Critter protection.** Line the bottom of your raised beds with hardware mesh. This product is similar to chicken wire or chicken fencing, but with much smaller openings, making it impossible for burrowing pests such as rats, mice, voles, and groundhogs to dig into your beds.

- **Secure the beds in place.** Dig a trench and drop your raised bed in it to help reduce the chance of shifting.

- **Choose thick boards.** When buying lumber, select boards that are at least 1.5" (3.8cm). Thicker boards will hold up longer than thin boards.

Don't forget about the paths. Paths and landings are important for safety, comfort, practicality, and aesthetic reasons. If being able to bring a wheelbarrow in between your beds is important to you, make sure that the paths are designed accordingly. In small urban gardens, I recommend 12"–18" (30cm–45cm) paths. Wood chips, pea gravel, and upcycled bricks are all good options for creating pathways. If you have the space to create brick or stone landings, I recommend it. A garden should be a place to relax. A landing or patio area will allow you to install some seating or an outdoor dining table, making the space enjoyable to all, even pets.

Filling New Raised Beds

Freshly constructed raised beds will require a significant amount of soil (bulk matter) and amendments to make them ready for use. My recommendation would be to source quality organic soil with compost or composted manure from a supplier in your area to bulk fill your beds. You can also purchase bags of triple mix and composted manure from your hardware store or garden center to bulk fill your beds. To further improve fertility and structure, mix in organic amendments such as worm castings, chicken manure pellets, kelp meal, and/or other commercial organic amendments.

The goal is to create a bed with loamy textured soil. This texture occurs when there are fairly equal parts of sand, silt, and clay in the growing medium. Loamy soil has good water holding capacity and doesn't compact, making it ideal for root development and overall plant health.

There are no limitations to what you can grow in a raised bed. Root crops, vining crops, and everything in between will grow and thrive in a raised bed. I would recommend avoiding perennial crops that tend to spread uncontrollably (like mint and lemon balm) unless you are dedicating an entire bed to them.

Important note, a raised bed that is built or installed on top of a concrete pad, pavers, or other material that blocks access to the native soil below should be treated like a container and not a raised bed.

Succession Planting

On a high level, succession planting is the process of continuously and strategically planting and/or transplanting crops to increase yields and spread out the harvest. On a granular level, succession planting can be implemented using different strategies that take into account the changing seasons, crop days to maturity, and yield quantities. The benefits of succession planting include:

- Maximizing the yield of your garden by leveraging your space efficiently
- Harvesting fresh and delicious homegrown produce regularly throughout the growing season
- Mitigating the risk of pest and disease pressure by growing an array of crops and varietals

Succession planting is as much an art as it is a science. Have fun with it, journal, and track your successes and failures.

Succession Planting with the Changing Seasons

One of the key ways to take advantage of succession planting and the changing seasons is to grow the right crops at the right time. The same square foot of soil can grow a spring (cool-weather) crop and a summer (warm-weather) crop. It can even be flipped again to grow a fall or winter (cool-weather) crop, depending on your zone.

If you are new to succession planting with the seasons, the best place to start is with a spring-to-summer crop transition. Rather than waiting for the weather to warm up so that you can plant your heat lovers come late spring, why not grow some crops that love cool weather and maximize the output from that same space?

- If you live in a region with a short spring, consider growing quickly maturing cool-weather crops like lettuce, radish, spinach, and Asian greens before transitioning to prized crops like tomatoes and peppers. If you were to grow carrots, beets, or brassicas, however, they would not mature quickly enough and your summer planting would be delayed.

- If you live in a region with a prolonged mild spring, you can consider growing cool-weather crops that take longer to mature before transitioning to summer crops.

Note: Transitioning from a summer to a fall crop is more complicated, and your likelihood of success will depend greatly on your climate, the long-range forecast, and your ability to protect these crops in the event of an early winter blast or a late fall warmup. My recommendation is to focus on maximizing your spring-to-summer succession and experimenting with a summer-to-fall transition to see what might work for you in your climate.

Here are a few examples to help you visualize how growing with the changing seasons can help maximize yields:

Spring Crop	Early Summer Crop	Mid-Summer Crop	Late Summer Crop	Fall Crop (or Winter crop)
Spinach (direct sow or transplant)	Tomatoes (transplant)			Spinach (transplant)
Radish (direct sow)	Peppers (transplant)			Baby lettuce (direct sow)
Peas (direct sow)		Beans (direct sow)		Lettuce – Head (transplant)
Carrots (direct sow)			Beets (direct sow or transplant)	

Succession Planting with Days to Maturity

An abundant garden provides sustenance regularly throughout the season. The days to maturity (DTM) vary from crop to crop and even from variety to variety. For example (see image), Tiara F1 cabbage has a DTM of 63 days, while Deadon cabbage has a DTM of 105 days. By growing different varieties of cabbage, you can stagger your harvest over several weeks. The same principle applies to potatoes, where you can grow early, mid-season, and late-season spuds. This is beneficial for several reasons since it helps reduce waste, keeps things interesting (as different varieties have different flavor profiles, colors, and textures), and helps ensure a steady harvest from week to week.

Succession Planting to Control Yields

Certain crops, especially cool-weather crops like arugula, radish, lettuce, and beets, have significant initial yields and will then either bolt or slow down entirely. They also have a very short harvest window. For example, a radish can turn from crunchy and delicious to pithy and unappetizing if not harvested at the ideal time. Lettuce will lose its sweet flavor and turn bitter if not harvested and enjoyed in the cool season. Although beets are more forgiving, they can become woody and unattractive rather quickly as the weather warms up and their days to maturity (DTM) date is passed.

These crops will benefit greatly from being successively grown every 7–10 days to ensure a steady harvest over several weeks. This technique involves leaving space in your garden that you can fill in over time. As crops are harvested and space is liberated, you can sow more of the same crop or change it up entirely. If you're on the cusp of a season change, consider switching from a cool-weather crop to a warm-weather crop (or vice versa).

If your goal is to preserve a large quantity of produce at once, such as by making pickled radishes or spinach smoothie bombs, then go ahead and sow what you need all at once. You do not need to succession plant in this case.

If you live in a region with an extended warm season, you can also succession plant warm-weather crops. Cucumber, summer squash, and beans are excellent crops for warm-weather succession planting, although if diseases are present in your garden, it may not be worth the effort. For example, if powdery mildew is affecting your first planting of summer squash, growing a second round might be a futile attempt. Young cucurbit seedlings will be susceptible to the same powdery mildew affecting their older more established siblings.

Direct sowing a row of radish seeds 10 days after the first row was planted.

Chapter 6

Fundamentals of Soil

The Importance of Soil Health

Feed your soil, and it will feed your soul. This is a concept that took me years to understand fully. For the uninitiated, soil is just dirt. But in reality, soil is much more. Soil is the source of life. It's a symphony; a complex and inspiring relationship between fauna and flora. It is where organic matter is transformed into nutrients that feed plants. Plants thrive and then provide food for wildlife. Organic matter is then returned to the soil, and the cycle continues.

The world of soil science can be broken into two fields of study. Pedology focuses on understanding and characterizing soil formation and evolution in the context of the natural environment. Edaphology focuses on how soil can influence living things such as plants. This field of study is incredibly important and complex, and that's why many books have been written on this topic. I will focus here on some key concepts and principles that will help you grow a healthy, abundant garden while respecting the soil and all it has to offer.

If you take anything away from this chapter, I hope it is the understanding that we owe our life to soil; specifically, topsoil. The upper layer of soil on Earth (the top 5–10 inches) has the highest concentration of organic matter and microorganisms. This is where most of the Earth's biological soil activity occurs, and as a result, it is responsible for feeding us. Humanity grows the vast majority of its food in this uppermost layer of soil. Without topsoil, our ability to feed ourselves diminishes greatly.

What can you do to help from a gardening perspective? Connect with the world around you. Connect with nature, the soil, the fauna, and the flora. You are part of a grand system, a cog in an immensely dynamic and vital machine. You are not more important than the cog beside you, nor is it more important than you. Treat your garden with the respect that it deserves, and it will repay you with abundance.

Micro and Macro Nutrients

Scientists have classified two main categories of essential plant nutrients (adding up to a total of 17 elements). Macronutrients are those nutrients that are needed in large quantities by plants. As the name suggests, micronutrients are important to overall plant health but are only needed in small quantities.

Furthermore, macronutrients can be classified as basic, primary, and secondary based on their importance to overall plant health. Carbon (C), oxygen (O), and hydrogen (H) are the most basic nutrients and are derived from air and water. Nitrogen (N), phosphorous (P), and potassium (K) are primary macronutrients, and I would say they are the most important nutrients to think about as a home gardener. Calcium (Ca), sulfur (S), and magnesium (Mg) are secondary macronutrients.

Micronutrients (a.k.a. trace minerals) include iron (Fe), boron (B), chlorine (Cl), manganese (Mn), zinc (Zn), copper (Cu), molybdenum (Mo), and nickel (Ni). Although these are important for overall plant success, unless there is a confirmed deficiency or problem in your soil, I wouldn't necessarily worry about them.

A note on soil tests: I have never felt the need to run a soil test. I focus on helping my soil remain healthy and thriving by supporting and amending it with organic matter. That being said, if you have concerns about your soil (due for example to previous improper use of the space, chemical spills, industrial usage of the land, and so on), consider having a certified lab run a soil test. This will help you discover any potential issues or ease your mind.

The primary macronutrients play a very important role. In fact, each one plays several roles and is responsible for various important functions. To simplify it, nitrogen (N) supports vegetative leaf growth, phosphorus (P) supports flowering and root formation, and potassium (K) supports overall plant health by encouraging the movement of nutrients, carbohydrates, and water in plant tissue.

Product Rundown

From a gardening perspective, it can be quite confusing to walk into a garden center or nursery and look at the different options for "soil" available to you. Some formulations are better suited for in-ground gardens, while other formulations are more appropriate for containers. I'll run down some of the common products you might find and their uses.

Topsoil: You will often find bags labeled topsoil in garden centers. These products can be used to create new garden beds when mixed with other organic materials like compost and/or composted manure. The challenge with these products is that they are not the most sustainable because they are mined or scraped from various locations, bagged, and resold to consumers.

Potting mix (sometimes called potting soil): A growing medium formulated for containers. It usually contains no topsoil at all. Different brands have different formulations, but they typically contain peat moss or coco coir with added perlite, vermiculite, compost, and other products like slow-release fertilizers. Organic options are available and recommended.

Seed starting mix: As the name suggests, it is a soilless product like potting mix that is used for seed starting. Formulated in much the same way as potting mix, it's usually screened so it's much finer than potting mix. A finer product allows seeds to germinate much more efficiently.

Compost: One of the best sources of organic matter, compost is created by decomposing organic matter like food waste into simpler organic and inorganic compounds. Compost can either be purchased or made. I certainly recommend that gardeners think about how they can repurpose their kitchen and garden waste to make compost. There are various systems available like tumblers, bokashi, and vermicomposting (also known as worm farming). I won't be going into detail on composting as this topic is quite expansive. It is, however, understandable that urban gardeners may not have the space to set up a composting system. Increasingly, municipalities have implemented composting and household organic waste collection. This creates compost that the city can use in public green spaces and/or distribute to residents.

Manure: This is composted animal waste, usually from sheep, cows, or horses. This product is used to amend garden beds and will typically contain other materials like animal bedding, rocks, and other debris. It can be used to amend beds in the spring and throughout the season as a top dressing.

Triple mix (3-way mix): This is a commercially packaged product that typically contains peat moss, compost, and topsoil.

Garden soil: This will vary by brand, and there are different formulations, but these products are meant to be used for in-ground beds. They usually contain a mix of topsoil and compost.

Worm castings: This is an organic form of fertilizer or soil amendment generated through vermicomposting; in other words, the waste produced by worms in the processing of organic matter such as garden and kitchen scraps. This is one of my favorite ways to add organic matter to garden beds. Commercial products are available on the market. Vermicomposting is an easy and fun way for the home gardener to create usable, nutrient-rich organic matter on-site by building a simple DIY system or purchasing a kit.

The takeaway: Learn what these various products are made of. Look at their ingredients so that you can make an informed decision about when and how to use them.

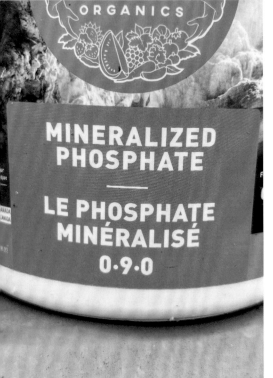

Amending Soil Organically

It is our responsibility as organic gardeners and good stewards of the land to replenish the nutrients that our plants have extracted from it to feed us. I think of this as keeping our end of the bargain with the soil that grows our food. My personal preference is to amend all my beds and containers in early spring, after the snow has melted and before I start my gardening season. This also allows me to assess how much organic matter I need to top up my beds.

My preferred organic amendments include compost, composted manure (sheep and/or cow), chicken manure pellets, worm castings, and commercial amendments for specific growing needs.

A note on commercially formulated amendments: Just like with fertilizers (Chapter 9), many if not all organic soil amendments have an NPK rating (nitrogen – phosphorus – potassium). The numbers refer to the proportion of each element found in the product. If you are not quite sure what you plan to grow in a given bed, you can use a balanced amendment (e.g., 4-4-4). If you plan to grow root crops in the bed, I would recommend amending with products higher in phosphorous (e.g., 0-9-0). For beds that will be used primarily for leafy greens, a nitrogen-rich amendment is recommended (e.g., 4-1-1). Use these numbers as a guideline because different suppliers will have different formulations.

Amending In-Ground Beds

Since we place so much emphasis on building up the soil, the last thing we want to do is overwork it. Over the last decade, I have adopted a no-till approach to gardening. I avoid tilling or disturbing the soil structure as much as possible. When it comes to in-ground beds, the best way to prepare them in the spring is to aerate them using a broadfork. This tool helps break up compacted or clay soil with minimal damage to soil structure. The process is simple enough: You use your body weight to drive the tines into the ground, repeating every few inches down the entire length of the bed. This can also be achieved with a standard garden fork. After aerating the soil, I recommend applying a 2" (5cm) layer of compost and/or manure and mixing in other sources of organic matter. You're now ready to plant.

Amending Raised Beds

When it comes to raised beds, you will notice that the soil level has sunk slightly in the spring. This is completely normal and to be expected. This is caused by settling that happens over time as well as depletion of organic matter in the soil over the growing season. I recommend using a combination of the following bulk materials to top off your beds to within 1" (2.5cm) of the top (stop there to avoid spillage): compost, composted manure, worm castings, chicken manure pellets, and specialty organic amendment. The same principles outlined previously on specific amendment formulations apply to raised beds as well.

Fundamentals of Soil

Amending Containers

When it comes to containers (e.g., pots, grow bags, gutter systems), I recommend using a specially formulated container mix. These products are "soilless" and contain a mélange of ingredients that support a plant's needs from both a structural and nutritional perspective. These mixes are also developed to hold the necessary amount of water and allow the rest to flow through. These products typically include slow-release fertilizers which are completely depleted by the end of the season. Therefore, reusing them as is the following year is not recommended as it can be counterproductive.

Ideally, you would use fresh potting mix every year, however, this is not economical or even practical. What would you do with all that old, depleted potting mix? I prefer to take a middle-of-the-road approach. When filling a container for planting, I combine 50% old potting mix with 50% new potting mix. I will also amend with an organic amendment appropriate for the intended crop. These containers will require frequent fertilization throughout the season (refer to Chapter 9).

If you are left with excess depleted potting mix, it can be added to raised or in-garden beds to bulk them up.

Mulching

Mulch provides multiple benefits in the vegetable garden:

- **Mulch feeds the soil.** Over time, organic mulches decompose and break down naturally. This adds beneficial nutrients to the soil and improves overall soil structure.

- **Mulch suppresses weeds.** A thick layer of mulch placed over bare soil helps reduce the chance of weed seeds germinating in the first place by depriving them of light. Mulch also acts as a physical barrier so any airborne seeds won't get a chance to reach the soil surface and germinate. Mulching helps suffocate existing weeds and allows your plants to establish themselves and thrive.

- **Mulch helps retain and regulate soil moisture.** Especially in hot climates, mulch helps soil retain moisture by reducing or limiting evaporation from the soil surface. Happy plants are healthy plants; keep your plants happy by preventing their roots from drying out. Reducing the chance of water stress is a key component to overall plant success.

- **Mulch regulates soil temperature.** This is key especially in spring and fall, when temperature swings tend to be significant. By mulching, we are essentially insulating the soil from unpredictable temperature variations that can stress the plants. We can't control the weather, but we can keep our soil comfortable.

There are several types of mulch on the market. I would strongly advise against using any synthetic or dyed mulches in the vegetable garden (such as rubber mulch or red/brown/black-dyed mulches). Choose organic options that will help your garden in the long run. My preferred mulch materials include:

- **Straw.** This is probably the most widely used mulch by vegetable gardeners. Choose organic or unsprayed straw if available.

- **Natural cedar mulch or bark.** This product consists of shredded or finely chopped cedar and is also a great product to use on garden paths.

- **Shredded leaves.** If you have mature trees on your property, then you're in luck. Leaves do take some time to break down, so it is recommended to shred them first. This can be done with a shredder or by simply running them over with a lawnmower a few times. They can be used directly in vegetable beds or flower beds. **Important note:** If the leaves are diseased, then I would recommend discarding them and not using them as mulch in your vegetable beds.

- **Compost.** Compost is not only a great soil amender, it can also be used as mulch. Throughout the season, top dress (apply around your plants and soil surface) with generous quantities of compost. Doing so not only helps to protect your soil, it also adds nutrients and organic matter to it. It's a win-win.

Do you need to apply mulch to your garden? The answer depends on several factors. If you are growing crops intensively and the soil surface is barely visible, then you probably don't need to bother with mulch. For example, a tightly planted bed of lettuce will eventually self-mulch. The lettuce heads will grow big enough to cover the soil surface entirely. Alternatively, in a tomato bed, you may want to consider mulching for several reasons, which may include moisture control, temperature control, and even disease prevention as outlined in Chapter 9. Aesthetics are an important part of urban gardening and should not be discounted. If the aesthetic of your garden is important to you, select a mulch material that you are comfortable with.

PEPPERS (HOT)

CHERRY TOMATOES

TOMATOES

SUMMER SQUASH

WINTER SQUASH

TOMATILLO/PHYSALIS

HERBS

FAVA

Johnny's
Selected Seeds
An employee-owned company

Certified Organic by MOFGA
Italian Eggplant

ROSA BIANCA OG,

Solanum melongena

2605G.11
PKT
DAYS 73

LOT 63604
MINIMUM 25 SEEDS

Germ: 99%
Germ Test Date: 10/19
Lot: 63604

2605G.11-63604

enton Avenue, Winslow, Maine 04901
77-564-6697 • Johnnyseeds.com

Johnny's
Selected Seeds
An employee-owned company

Hybrid Italian Eggplant
NU

Solar

657.11
MINIMUM 25 SEED
DAYS 68

Johnny's
Selected Seeds
An employee-owned company

Hybrid Asian Eggplant
ASIAN DELITE F1,

Solanum melongena

LOT 70238

4413.11
MINIMUM 25 SEEDS
DAYS 60

955 Benton Avenue, Winslow, Maine 04901
1-877-564-6697 • Johnnyseeds.com

4413.11-70238

The downside to open-pollinated varieties is that they may not be as resistant to disease or pests as some of the specialty hybrids available on the market.

Heirloom Seeds

Costoluto Genovese Tomato, an Italian heirloom variety that is said to have been in production since the nineteenth century.

Heirlooms are "old world" open-pollinated varieties that have existed for many years, passed down from one generation of gardeners and farmers to the next, because of their distinctive qualities (including taste, shape, or growth habit). Although there isn't a set standard that is internationally recognized, for a variety to be considered an heirloom, it must be stable and have been cultivated for many years. Some say 50 years is sufficient to grant a variety the heirloom label, while others say 100 years is the minimum. Heirloom varieties are open-pollinated, but not all open-pollinated varieties are necessarily heirlooms. Some of my favorite varieties are heirlooms. Refer to the crop guides for my preferred varieties.

Hybrid Seeds

Tiara F1 Cabbage, a hybrid bred for compact growth habit.

Hybrids are varieties that have been specifically bred for certain traits like disease resistance, fruit shape, color, growth habit, high yield, or other characteristics.

Many people confuse hybrid seeds with GMO (Genetically Modified Organisms) seeds. Hybrids are produced by crossing two plants to produce offspring that have desirable traits. Typically, the name of the variety will be followed by an F1 label, meaning first-generation hybrid seed or plant bred via the successful cross-pollination of two parent plants. Whenever I explain this to someone, I like to use the analogy of dog breeding. A Labradoodle is a dog bred by mating a Labrador Retriever with a Standard, Miniature or Toy Poodle. The result is still a cute and loveable pet, not a sort of abomination.

Hybrids can come about in different ways. They can be created accidentally. For example, planting two varieties of the same crop family close to each other may result in fruit with hybrid seeds. They can also be created deliberately by human intervention. Many seed companies have breeding programs. Just like any business, they want to provide their customers with new and exciting varieties.

Some hybrids are patented by their owners, so you are legally bound not to save their seed or else you'll be in violation of their intellectual property rights. It is important to make sure that your passion for gardening doesn't turn into a potential headache. While hybrids are created through selective breeding (crossing plant A with plant B), GMOs tend to be produced using high-tech methods (gene splicing). The distinction here is that GMOs are varieties that do not occur naturally, whereas hybrids come to be through selective breeding. It is important to note that currently GMO seeds are not available to home gardeners. Only commercial farmers can purchase GMO seeds; common GMO seeds include canola, soybeans, corn, and sugar beets.

Certified Organic Seeds

As the name suggests, seeds that include this label are certified by a governing body in the jurisdiction where they are produced and/or sold. This means that the seeds were collected from plants grown according to specified standards. Think of this as an additional layer of quality when shopping for seeds.

It is important to note that obtaining such designations can be a logistical and bureaucratic nightmare for some growers. Just because a seed packet doesn't have a certified organic label on it does not mean that the grower did not follow organic principles. When in doubt, contact the supplier and ask them. I have found that many small-scale seed suppliers are willing to talk to you about their process.

Determinate vs. Indeterminate Varieties

This designation will apply primarily to tomatoes but can also apply to other crops as well. Tomatoes evolved as vining plants (indeterminate), meaning they can grow several feet tall and continue to produce off-shoots (a.k.a. suckers), which then, in turn, start producing flowers and fruit.

Determinate (also referred to as bush or patio) varieties are bred not to vine uncontrollably like indeterminate varieties. They are ideal for container gardens or if you don't have much space to work with;

they're also ideal for areas where the hot summer growing season is short. They tend to set all their fruit at once and then they are done for the season.

Direct Sow or Direct Seed

These terms can refer either to seeds that prefer to be planted directly into the garden or to the method of directly seeding a crop in the garden. This is the simplest way to grow food, and it's what we visualize when we think of growing an edible garden. When you directly sow a seed into the ground, it will germinate and grow in place. There is no transplanting required. There are a few reasons why you would want to consider direct sowing:

1. **Certain crop families prefer not to be transplanted.** These include root vegetables such as radishes, carrots, and turnips.

2. **Reducing transplant shock.** Some crop families can experience severe transplant shock, meaning that if you disturb their roots in any way, their growth may slow down and it could take days for them to recover. Crops in the cucurbit family are prone to transplant shock. Although these crops can be started indoors, in my experience, they tend to perform best when directly sown.

3. **Eliminating the need to harden off.** The process of hardening off and its importance in the indoor seed starting process are covered in Chapter 8.

4. **More economical.** By sowing directly outdoors, you eliminate the need to start seeds indoors and the associated costs that this incurs.

When direct sowing, it is important to follow the guidelines on the seed packet for planting depth and germinating temperature. The rule of thumb is that the larger the seed, the deeper it needs to be sown.

Days to Maturity (DTM)

Days to maturity refers to the number of days it will take for a crop to be ready to harvest after it has been transplanted into the ground. This number should be viewed more as a guideline than a firm timeline, since it is based on ideal growing conditions. This number will be printed on seed packets and listed on supplier websites. It will vary greatly not only based on crop type but also crop variety. I don't rely on this number to tell me when I can expect to start harvesting. I prefer to use the number to help me plan my garden and crop placement so that I can best take advantage of strategic planting techniques like succession planting (see Chapter 5).

Germination Rate

As part of their quality assurance practices, seed suppliers will conduct germination tests on their seed stocks. This helps the supplier (and the consumer) understand how viable seeds are. For example, a 90% germination rate indicates that out of 10 seeds sown, 9 will germinate. This information is useful when starting seeds indoors and when direct sowing. It allows us to sow additional (or "buffer") seeds as discussed in Chapter 8.

Should You Start from Seed?

To start from seed or not to start from seed? That is the question. Every spring, when the catalogs start showing up in my mailbox, I get a little giddy, as I'm sure many of you do as well. There are so many beautiful and new varieties with vibrant colors and unique shapes. I want to start by saying that indoor seed starting is not for everyone. If you are a new gardener without much experience in plant care and maintenance, I would encourage you not to embark on an indoor seed starting project during your first year. Instead, focus your efforts on seedlings and direct sow crops.

Why you should start seeds indoors:

- **Exploring new varieties.** Starting seeds allows you to select particular crops and varietals. You can grow rare and unique varieties that are not typically available at your local garden center and nursery (which generally produce seedlings for the mass market).

- **Understanding the process.** If you have an interest in plant science, germination, plant care, and maintenance, then seed starting can certainly offer you an opportunity to observe and learn about this important process.

Why you should consider buying seedlings from the nursery or garden center:

- **Lower cost.** If you have a small garden and only need to grow a few seedlings, the cost of acquiring all the necessary seed starting equipment may not make sense financially compared to simply buying quality organic seedlings.

- **Availability and time restrictions.** If you plan to travel or don't have the time to monitor seedlings you start from seed, it may be best to rely on expert growers for your seedlings come spring.

There is absolutely no shame in purchasing seedlings from a grower or nursery. Doing so doesn't make you any less of a gardener. When shopping for seedlings, I recommend sourcing from reputable suppliers or garden centers that you trust. Choose organically grown seedlings if possible. There are certain crops that I always recommend you purchase as seedlings because they are difficult to start yourself. These include woody herbs like sage, rosemary, thyme, and oregano. I also prefer to purchase strawberry plants or bare roots rather than starting from seed. Next, I will cover the crops that I recommend you buy as seedlings, the ones I recommend you direct sow, and the ones I recommend you start indoors.

Planting Guide

It can be quite confusing for a new (or even a seasoned) gardener to decide when, how, where, and why to grow certain crops. As outlined in Chapter 4, crops can be divided into two primary categories, warm-weather crops and cool-weather crops. Warm-weather crops are those that thrive in the heat of summer; they are typically planted out after the last frost (in an area where frost occurs) and when nighttime temperatures are at or above 50°F/10°C. These include favorites like tomatoes, peppers, eggplants, beans, and basil, to name a few. Cool-weather crops prefer the milder temperatures of spring and fall (or winter, if you live in a region that does not experience freezing temperatures). They are typically planted out when nighttime temperatures are at or above 39°F/4°C. Cool-weather crops include cabbage, broccoli, radish, spinach, and cilantro among others. (More information on transplanting can be found in Chapter 8.)

Furthermore, certain crops prefer to be directly sown outdoors while others need time to grow indoors before being transplanted out. The following table provides a fairly wide-ranging list of common crops and their preferences, including some beneficial flowers that work well in the edible garden. Note that this list is based on my personal experience and what has worked for me in my urban garden. There is certainly wiggle room with these numbers in either direction. Use these numbers as general guidelines.

A note on containers: Most crops will in fact grow in a container, but whether or not they will thrive is usually dependent on several factors. I have indicated which crops are likely to thrive in containers and my recommendations for container size and the number of plants per container. There is wiggle room here as well. Plants are incredibly resilient and want to grow, even in less than favorable conditions.

Crop	Planting Method (Direct Sow or Transplant)	Will it thrive in cool or warm weather?	Will thrive in a container?	Minimum Container Size (gallons)	Number of plants per container
Arugula	Both	Cool Weather	Yes	5	Multiple
Beans	Direct Sow	Warm Weather	Yes (bush beans only)	7	4
Beets	Both	Cool Weather	Yes	15*	10
Bok Choy	Both	Cool Weather	Yes	10	4-6
Borage	Both	Warm Weather	No	-	-
Broccoli	Transplant	Cool Weather	Yes	15	1
Brussels Sprouts	Transplant	Cool Weather	No	-	-
Cabbage	Transplant	Cool Weather	No	-	-
Carrots	Direct Sow	Cool Weather	Yes (deep container)	20	30-40**
Cauliflower	Transplant	Cool Weather	No	-	-
Celery	Transplant	Cool Weather	No	-	-
Collards	Both	Cool Weather	Yes	5	1
Corn	Both	Warm Weather	No	-	-
Cosmos	Both	Warm Weather	Yes	10	1-2
Cucamelon	Both	Warm Weather	No	-	-
Cucumber	Both	Warm Weather	Yes (patio or bush varieties only)	7	2
Eggplant	Transplant	Warm Weather	Yes	7	1

Crop	Planting Method (Direct Sow or Transplant)	Will it thrive in cool or warm weather?	Will thrive in a container?	Minimum Container Size (gallons)	Number of plants per container
Garlic	Direct Sow	Fall Planting	No	-	-
Ground Cherry	Transplant	Warm Weather	No	-	-
Kale	Both	Cool Weather	Yes	5	1
Kohlrabi	Both	Cool Weather	Yes	15	5
Leek	Transplant	Cool Weather	No	-	-
Lettuce - Baby Leaf	Direct Sow	Cool Weather	Yes	5	Multiple
Lettuce - Head	Both	Cool Weather	Yes	5	2
Marigold	Transplant	Warm Weather	Yes	5	1
Melon	Transplant	Warm Weather	No	-	-
Mustard Greens	Both	Cool Weather	Yes	5	1
Nasturtium	Both	Warm Weather	Yes	5	3
Okra	Both	Warm Weather	No	-	-
Onion	Transplant	Cool Weather	No	-	-
Pansy	Transplant	Cool Weather	Yes	5	1-3
Parsnip	Direct Sow	Cool Weather	No	-	-
Peas	Direct Sow	Cool Weather	Yes (dwarf only)	10	4
Pepper	Transplant	Warm Weather	Yes	7	1
Potatoes	Direct Sow	Cool Weather	Yes (tall bags)	15	3***
Radish	Direct Sow	Cool Weather	Yes (shallow and wide)	15*	Multiple

Crop	Planting Method (Direct Sow or Transplant)	Will it thrive in cool or warm weather?	Will thrive in a container?	Minimum Container Size (gallons)	Number of plants per container
Spinach	Both	Cool Weather	Yes (shallow and wide)	15	Multiple
Strawberry	Consider purchasing seedlings	Cool Weather	Yes (shallow and wide)	15	Multiple
Sunflowers	Direct Sow	Warm Weather	Yes (dwarf types only)	10	Multiple****
Swiss Chard	Both	Cool Weather	Yes	5	1
Tomatillo	Transplant	Warm Weather	Yes	10	1
Tomatoes	Transplant	Warm Weather	Yes	10	1
Turnip - Tokyo	Direct Sow	Cool Weather	Yes	15*	Multiple
Turnip	Direct Sow	Cool Weather	Yes	15*	8-10
Winter Squash	Both	Warm Weather	No	-	-
Zinnia	Both	Warm Weather	Yes	10	1-2
Zucchini	Both	Warm Weather	No	-	-

* Root crops such as beets, radishes, and turnips prefer wider containers, which allow for more seeds to be sown. Container height should be at least 10" (25cm) tall for beets and turnips and 6" (15cm) for radishes and Tokyo turnips.

** Carrots should be heavily sown and then thinned down. Refer to the carrot crop guide in Chapter 2 for more information.

*** Potatoes will grow in a tall container or grow bag. Three seed potatoes per 15 gallons of soil volume is the ratio that works best.

**** Dwarf sunflowers come in a range of options. Consult the seed packet for optimal variety-specific spacing and other requirements.

Crop	Perennial/ Biennial/ Annual and hardiness	Planting Method (direct sow or transplant)	Will it thrive in a container?	Minimum Container Size (gallons)	Number of plants per container
Basil	Annual *	Transplant	Yes	5	Multiple
Calendula	Annual *	Both	Yes	5	1
Chamomile (German)	Annual *	Transplant	Yes	5	1
Chives	Perennial Zone 3–10	Consider purchasing seedlings	Yes	3	1 (1 cluster of chives)
Cilantro	Annual *	Both	Yes	5	Multiple
Dill	Annual *	Both	Yes	5	Multiple
Lavender	Perennial	Consider purchasing seedlings	Yes **	5	1
Mint	Perennial Zone 3–8	Consider purchasing seedlings	Yes	5	1
Oregano	Perennial Zones 5–10	Consider purchasing seedlings	Yes	3	1
Parsley	Biennial *** Zone 3–9	Transplant	Yes	5	1–3
Rosemary	Perennial ****	Consider purchasing seedlings	Yes	5	1
Sage	Perennial Zone 5–8	Consider purchasing seedlings	Yes	3	1
Thyme	Perennial Zone 5–9	Consider purchasing seedlings	Yes	3	1

I broke out the herbs into a separate table as they are treated somewhat differently. Some herbs are perennial in certain zones and do not need to be replanted. Other herbs are biennial (meaning that they flower in their second year).

The table across includes a list of common culinary herbs and flowers as well as their hardiness. Information about herb hardiness is spotty at best, and you will often find contradictory information online. Rather than focusing solely on zone numbers, the table is meant to give you an overview of various culinary herbs and whether or not they will likely thrive in your garden.

Disclaimer: Varieties within a plant species may have differing hardiness levels. It is important to find variety-specific information on hardiness from seed and seedling suppliers. As discussed in Chapter 4, microclimates can play a significant role in a plant's hardiness. Growing perennial herbs in containers is possible and can be quite rewarding. However, special care must be taken to protect potted perennial herbs over the winter. See Chapter 10 for more information on winterization.

* Annual herbs might self-seed if allowed to flower. Seeds may form and drop to the ground, resulting in new plants the same year or the next year. But relying on annual herbs self-seeding for the next year is not a good idea since there are no guarantees the seeds will germinate and grow. I recommend starting with new annual herb seedlings every season. Consider any volunteer herbs that pop up as bonus plants.

** Certain varieties of lavender are more suitable for containers. Select dwarf or compact varieties.

*** As a biennial, parsley will flower in its second year. I recommend starting with new parsley seedlings every season.

**** Rosemary is a perennial herb. However, I treat it as an annual in my garden. There are many varieties of rosemary, and some claim to be hardy in zone 5. In my experience, this is not quite the case. Rosemary does well as a perennial in warmer climates.

Chapter 8

Seed Starting for Beginners

One of the most rewarding garden activities is without a doubt starting seeds. As mentioned earlier, I do not recommend seed starting if you are new to gardening in general. But if you do want to embark on a seed starting project, this chapter should help set you off on the right path.

I don't own a greenhouse, and even if I did, it would have to be heated for me to be able to use it to start seeds in late winter. Therefore, I start seeds indoors, in the comfort of my own home, where the temperature is consistent and I have full control of the growing environment.

Equipment

I have broken up the list of equipment needed into two parts: seed starting materials and grow shelving materials. Note that these supplies can easily be found at your local hardware store, garden centers, hydroponic stores, and online.

Grow Shelving Materials

- Shelving unit with adjustable height racks. Four-foot-wide units are ideal.
- Grow lights. I do not use commercially marketed grow lights. I prefer to use 4-foot-long LED Shop Lights (the same width as the shelving unit).
- Heat mats (to aid in germinating warm-weather crops)
- Extension cords
- Mechanical timer
- Pieces of scrap wood or piping and zip ties (to attach lights)
- Chains, C-hooks, and S-hooks (used to control and adjust the height of the light strips)
- Small portable fan

Seed Starting Materials

- Growing medium: My preference is to use a commercial sterile organic seed starting mix.
- Seed starting trays, also known as 1020 trays because of their standard 10" x 20" size
- Cell pack sheets or plug trays: There are a few options to choose from, but starting with 30–40 holes per tray is recommended.
- Humidity domes: These help retain moisture and aid in germination—choose short humidity domes no taller than 2" (5cm).
- Seeds
- Labels
- Watering can and spray bottle

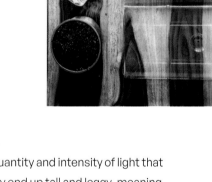

As your seedlings grow, you will need the following supplies:

- Organic fertilizer
- Larger containers for potting up (e.g., 4" pots)
- Yellow sticky traps in case you have flies or fungus gnats

An important note on window light: A window does not provide the quantity and intensity of light that germinating seeds require to grow into healthy seedlings. Seedlings may end up tall and leggy, meaning the plants will be weak, and can potentially fail, ruining the entire seed starting project. Supplementing with artificial light is critical for success.

When shopping for LED shop lights, the most important specification to look out for is the Kelvin rating. A Kelvin is a unit of measurement used to describe the hue of a light source. The lower the Kelvin value, the warmer or more yellow the color; the higher the Kelvin value, the closer the hue is to daylight. My recommendation is to use LED light at 6000–6500K. Descriptions like "daylight" or "cool light" may be included on the package label or listing. This range replicates daylight, which is exactly what seedlings need in the vegetative state as they grow and put on new leaves.

These LED shop lights are linkable, allowing you to get creative with how you arrange them. You can choose to have 3 or 4 lights per shelf depending on how you plan to position your seedlings. Attach them directly to a piece of scrap wood or PVC piping and add C-hooks. Attach chains directly to the shelving unit using an S-hook, and hook the bottom of the chain to the C-hook on the PVC or scrap wood piece holding the light.

You can control the light source by adjusting the chains. Alternatively, you can attach the lights directly to the shelves using zip ties and adjust the shelf height as your seedlings grow.

Important note: These types of lights are not suitable for fruiting or flowering plants. Since the goal with indoor seed starting projects is to give plants an opportunity to grow into healthy seedlings rather than to flower and fruit indoors, the lights recommended here will work well. If your goal is to continue growing these plants indoors into the fruiting stage, you may require different light systems, and I would encourage you to contact a local hydroponic store for advice and product recommendations.

How long should you keep the lights on while your seedlings grow indoors? As seeds germinate and emerge, leave the lights on for 16 hours. This is where the mechanical timer comes into play. Two to three weeks before it's time to move your seedlings outside, begin to decrease the time the lights are on, eventually ending up with around 12 hours a day of light.

 Scan the QR code to watch a video of my seed starting shelving unit and light setup.

My Seed Starting Technique

There are different ways to start seeds. What I describe below is the technique I have used successfully for years.

1. Prepare your growing medium by wetting it, but do not overdo it. You'll know that it is sufficiently damp when you're able to compress it into a ball in your hand and easily break it apart when you poke at it. Sterile growing media can be quite hydrophobic, meaning that they don't absorb water readily and require some coaxing and time to become adequately moistened. This is normal; simply take your time, and the medium will eventually absorb water.

2. Fill your cell packs or plugs with moist growing medium by pressing down firmly, but not too hard. If you compress the medium too much, the roots will struggle to get established. Fill the cell packs or plugs about 90% of the way.

3. Sow your seeds. Follow seed packet instructions for planting depth. The general rule of thumb is that the bigger the seed, the deeper it needs to be sown. For larger seeds that need to be sown deeper, you can use a dibber or pen to create the necessary room to push the seed down.

Seed Insurance

This refers to the practice of planting extra seeds in each single cell to compensate for low germination rates. The idea here is that you're guaranteeing at least one seed will germinate in that cell. I will typically sow 2–3 seeds per cell and thin to a single seedling later on for crops that grow as a single plant like tomatoes, peppers, and eggplants. You do not need to thin crops that can grow in bunches or clumps, such as onions, baby lettuce, or mesclun.

4. Cover your seeds with more growing medium to achieve the desired sowing depth, press down gently, and level off. Your cell packs should now be full of growing medium all the way to the rim. Place the cell packs inside the 1020 trays. Now would be a good time to add your labels.

5. Mist the trays with a spray bottle and cover them with a humidity dome.

6. Place the tray on the seed starting shelf under the grow lights. Although the trays do not generally require light until the seeds have germinated, it is good practice to have the lights on right away. This prevents the emerging seedlings from getting leggy in the event that you forget to check on them and turn the light on when needed. Make sure that there is no more than 2" (5cm) of clearance from the top of your seed starting tray to the light source.

7. If needed, use a heat mat to help with germination. Warm-weather crops like tomatoes and peppers will benefit from additional heat to germinate, especially if your seed-starting setup is in a colder part of your home. Place the entire seed tray on a heat mat with the humidity dome on top. **Note:** Cool-weather crops do not need heat to germinate. Excess heat may be counterproductive. Skip the heat mat for all cool-weather crops, including lettuce, brassicas, and Asian greens.

8. Check on your seed trays every couple of days. Keep the growing medium surface moist by misting it with a spray bottle. Avoid using a watering can because this can disturb the seeds and cause the medium to slosh around.

9. Once the seeds germinate, remove the dome and the heat mat (if using).

If you followed all of the steps outlined above, your seeds should germinate and begin to emerge within a few days. Germination time will vary from crop to crop, and even from variety to variety. Your seed packets should give you an indication of how many days it takes for a given seed to germinate. Not every seed sown will grow into a seedling, as mentioned in the seed insurance discussion earlier. Avoid poking at your growing medium. The light source needs to be within 2" (5cm) of your seedling. As your seedlings grow taller, either lift the light source by a notch or two on the chain, or adjust your shelf height accordingly.

 Scan the QR code to watch a live demonstration of my seed starting process.

Thinning vs. Separating Seedlings

The first leaves that appear are called cotyledon. They do not have the same shape as your plant's "true" leaves. Once your seedlings have produced their first set of true leaves, you will be faced with a choice. Depending on how many seeds you sowed, the germination rate, and your desired result, you will probably need to thin your seedlings down to one seedling per cell. For example, tomato, pepper, eggplant, brassica, and head lettuce seedlings should be thinned to one plant per cell. Looseleaf lettuce, baby green mixes, and other intensely planted crops do not need to be thinned.

Thinning involves snipping away excess seedlings from a cell, leaving behind the healthiest and most robust seedlings. This is a controversial practice that is viewed as wasteful by some. However, it is the easiest method for a new gardener. Alternatively, you can carefully separate the seedlings by teasing the roots apart and repotting. The separating and repotting process is best performed when you are repotting your seedlings into a larger container (see next section in this chapter).

The following table is a reasonably comprehensive list of crops with sowing recommendations based on my experience and what has worked for me. It's a starting point. There's wiggle room in either direction. For example, if you are using older seeds and you're not confident in their germination potential, you can be more conservative with your seed insurance by sowing a few more. If you have brand-new seeds from a supplier you trust, you can sow fewer seeds.

Crop	Number of seeds per cell to start	Should you thin or separate to a single seedling per cell or pot?	Requires potting up to larger container?
Arugula	Multiple	No	No
Basil	4–6	Optional	Possibly
Beets	3–4	No *	No
Bok Choy	2–3	Yes	No
Broccoli	2–3	Yes	Possibly
Brussels Sprouts	2–3	Yes	Possibly
Cabbage	2–3	Yes	Possibly
Calendula	2–3	Yes	No
Cauliflower	2–3	Yes	Possibly
Celery	4–5	Yes	Possibly
Chamomile	5–6	Yes	No
Cilantro	4–5	Optional	No
Collards	2–3	Yes	Possibly
Corn	1–2	Yes	No
Cucamelon	2–3	Yes	No
Cucumber	2–3	Yes	No
Dill	3–4	Optional	No
Eggplant	2–3	Yes	Yes
Ground Cherry	2–3	Yes	Possibly
Kale	2–3	Yes	Possibly
Kohlrabi	2–3	Yes	Possibly
Leek	Multiple	No **	No
Lettuce – head	2–3	Yes	No
Marigold	2–3	Yes	No
Melon	1–2	Yes	Possibly ***
Mustard Greens	2–3	Yes	No
Nasturtium	1–2	Optional	No
Okra	1–2	Yes	Possibly
Onion	Multiple	No **	No

Crop	Number of seeds per cell to start	Should you thin or separate to a single seedling per cell or pot?	Requires potting up to larger container?
Parsley	4–5	Optional	No
Pepper	2–3	Yes	Yes
Spinach	4–5	Optional	No
Swiss Chard	2–3	Optional, but recommended	No
Tomatillo	2–3	Yes	Yes
Tomatoes	2–3	Yes	Yes
Winter Squash	1–2	Yes	Possibly ***
Zucchini	1–2	Yes	Possibly ***

Crops marked with "Multiple" can be densely sown.

* Beetroots can be multi-sown and transplanted where they will continue to grow in clumps. This method works well for gardeners with limited access to space.

** Allium seedlings such as onions, leeks, and shallots are only separated at planting time. Their roots are very robust, and seedlings can be separated quite easily.

*** Consider starting melons, zucchini, and squash in a larger pot from the start as they tend to grow quickly and vigorously. They also do not like to have their roots disturbed, and this would avoid the need to pot up to a larger container.

Caring for Your Seedlings

Watering

Watering might seem straightforward enough, but in reality, people often make a couple of big watering mistakes when starting seeds. Overwatering and watering from above are the leading causes of seed starting failure. We tend to instinctively think of watering a plant by pouring water on the soil in which it grows. This is what we have been taught from a young age. The problem with this as a technique, especially with young and delicate seedlings, is that it can create favorable conditions for damping off (a fungal disease that leads to rot of the plant stem) to occur. It can also create an environment for fungus gnats to breed.

Watering from below is a more appropriate method. By allowing your cells, plugs, or containers to absorb water from the bottom up, the plant and growing medium will wick water up slowly and in adequate quantities. This is critical in the early growth stages when the plant stems are still weak and tender. This also helps reduce the chance of damping off.

There are several ways to do this, but the way I do it is by pouring water directly into the 1020 tray. Then I check back on the tray in 30 minutes. If the water has been absorbed fully, I will typically add more water and check back in another 30 minutes. I always err on the side of caution when watering. It is better to under water than overwater.

Eventually, you'll start relying on your gut and know how much water the seedlings need by feeling the weight of the tray and noticing visual cues. This skill takes time to hone, so don't beat yourself up over it. All good things take time.

Fertilizing

If you used a good quality organic seed starting mix, it should already come preloaded with nutrients to help your seedlings thrive. However, your seedlings may need an additional boost while they are still indoors waiting to be moved outside. Generally speaking, the crops that may need additional feeding will be the ones that require at least six weeks of indoor growing, such as tomatoes, peppers, eggplants, and certain flowers. Crops that only need a short indoor growing period, like lettuces and Asian greens, do not need to be fed.

Since your seedlings are in a "vegetative state" during the starting process—meaning they are growing foliage, not flowers—the fertilizer you use should be higher in nitrogen (N) and low in phosphorous (P) and potassium (K). I use an organic fish emulsion or seaweed fertilizer, which I dilute to half the strength normally used if you were feeding established plants out in the garden. I prepare the mix in a watering can and bottom water the cell packs, plugs, and containers from below, the same way I usually water my seedlings.

Potting Up

The term "potting up" refers to repotting your seedlings into a larger container. The goal is to ensure that the plants have enough room to stretch their roots and continue to establish themselves. Seedlings can become root-bound quite quickly, especially if started in small cell packs or plugs. You should monitor the root structure, and at the first sign that your seedlings are becoming root-bound (i.e., roots are circling themselves), move the seedlings up to a larger pot.

As I mentioned earlier, I like to start my seeds in cell packs. This allows me to start 30–40 plants in one tray. Some crops can live happily in these cell packs until it's time to transplant. These include quick-growing crops that only need to be started a few weeks before your last frost date (e.g., lettuce, arugula, salad mixes, beets, and others). However, for slower-growing crops that need to be started much earlier, including tomatoes, peppers, and eggplants, you will need to pot up. You may even need to pot up a few times, depending on how quickly your seedlings grow. A good time to consider potting up is when your seedlings have their second set of true leaves.

Some crops can grow new roots from their stems. Examples include tomatoes, tomatillos, and to a lesser extent, peppers. When it is time to pot up these seedlings, I bury some of the stem to encourage more root growth. More roots mean healthier plants.

When potting up, I prefer to use fresh container or potting mix. I do not use seed starting mix when potting up for several reasons. By weight, seed starting mix tends to be more expensive than standard potting mix. Seed starting mix also doesn't provide the same nutritional benefits as standard potting mix when seedlings are more mature. When potting up, it is possible to use a custom mix of compost, perlite, vermiculite, and coco coir. I do not mix my own container mix and prefer to rely on reputable suppliers.

 Scan the QR code to watch a video of me potting up seedlings.

Monitoring your Seedlings for Pests and Disease

It can be quite disheartening to spend time and money on a seed starting project only to be faced with mold, gnats, or other issues. Unfortunately, this is part of the organic gardening process. We do our best to prevent issues, but sometimes, what happens can be completely out of our control.

To help mitigate the risk of pests and disease, follow these basic guidelines:

- Use quality organic growing media.
- Water from below, always. Resist the urge to water from above.
- If you spot fungus gnats, deploy yellow sticky traps around your seed starting station.

Circulating the Air

Running a small fan to help circulate the air around your seedlings is a good idea for several reasons:

- The air helps keep the surface of your growing medium dry, which reduces the likelihood of fungus gnats.

- Blowing air also helps reduce the likelihood of damping off by keeping the surface of the growing medium dry.

- The air will help cool down your lights, which can emit quite a bit of heat throughout the day.

- Air simulates wind, which helps your seedlings establish stronger stems. You are essentially preparing your seedlings for the outside world by acclimating them to the conditions they will face.

I recommend using a small room fan and positioning it in different directions as needed. The goal is to get your seedlings moving. I will typically run the fan for 1–2 hours a day, sometimes more, sometimes less. There's no need to run it continuously. Start running the fan after your seedlings have their first set of true leaves. This practice is important, but if you forget to do it for a day or two, don't panic. Plants are incredibly resilient.

Hardening Off Process

Hardening off is an essential part of the seed starting process. It involves the gradual exposure of your seedlings to the outside elements so that they can get accustomed to the outside world. If you were to take a seedling that lived its entire existence in the comfort of your house and plant it out without this gradual exposure, you risk losing the seedling altogether. We certainly don't want that, not after spending time, money, and effort all these weeks nurturing these seedlings.

There is no hard science here, but this is what I do. I make sure I'll be home the week I harden off my plants. On day 1, I move the trays out to a sheltered spot for 1 hour. On day 2, I move the trays out to a sheltered spot for 2 hours. Day 3: 3 hours. On day 4, I'll give them some direct sun. By day 7, they will spend 7 hours per day outdoors with sun exposure. I may even leave them out overnight if the temperature is suitable.

If possible, the trays should be moved under the grow lights when they are brought back inside. However, this isn't necessary. My seed starting setup is on my second floor, and moving trays up and down daily is very cumbersome. By the time you begin hardening off, your seedlings should already be healthy and established, so a few days without artificial light won't harm them.

Since different plants are transplanted outside at different times, I do not harden off everything the same week. In spring, cold-hardy crops get transplanted first. Therefore, I'll harden those off first. A few weeks later, I'll start hardening off my warm-weather crops. You will have to keep an eye on the forecast and your specific growing zone requirements.

Transplanting into the Garden

Your seedlings are hardened off and ready to be planted outdoors. Seems straightforward enough, but there are some important considerations to take into account at this stage. If you have not already done so, amend your beds and containers as outlined in Chapter 6 to get them ready to receive the seedlings.

Come spring, any gardener will be itching to get out there and plant. However, if seedlings are transplanted either too early or too late, it could spell disaster. To avoid disappointment, consider the following guidelines:

- Cool-weather crops should be transplanted out when the nighttime lows are at least 39°F/4°C and the soil is workable. Be ready to cover your crops with frost cloth or row cover in case there's a major dip in temperature or an unexpected snowfall.

- Warm-weather crops should be transplanted out when the nighttime lows average at least 50°F/10°C and the soil temperature is 60°F/15°C. Invest in a soil thermometer.

- Consider spacing, light requirements, plant positioning, and how the plants will look at maturity. Refer to the planting guide in Chapter 7.

Keep an eye on the long-range forecast. This is especially important when planting out warm-weather crops because they can be severely impacted by a late cooldown in temperature. A general rule of thumb is to wait at least 2 weeks after your last average frost date to transplant your warm-weather crops. I recommend referring to your seed supplier website or seed packet as it may include additional information on transplant timing.

Most cool-weather seedlings started indoors (including lettuces, kale, and Asian greens) should be planted without burying the stem. It is important to plant your seedlings so that the soil level matches the seedling growing medium. The same procedure applies to warm-weather crops, with a couple of exceptions.

Tomatoes: For optimal results, you should consider burying some of the stem when transplanting. Tomato stems root, meaning they will shoot out new roots from the stem when they touch moist growing media. This results in a healthy and well-established plant. Strip off some of the bottom leaves, dig a deep hole in the garden bed or container, place your seedling, and backfill with more growing medium. Make sure to leave the top of the plant exposed above the soil line so it can keep growing. In other words, don't bury the whole plant. Tomatillos also benefit from this.

Optional: When transplanting your seedlings, you can consider using a mycorrhizal inoculant. These commercial products can help your seedlings develop stronger root systems, increasing the plant's ability to absorb nutrients.

Chapter 9

Garden Maintenance

A neglected garden is not a thriving and abundant garden. Growing food is not a hands-off activity. I encourage you to spend as much time in your garden as you can. Observe your plants and look for signs of stress or disease. Get up close and personal and search for pests. Trust me, when you take an active role in the garden, it will thank you and reward you with bountiful harvests and beautiful flowers.

For me, garden maintenance boils down to the following:

- Keep garden paths and beds weed-free and clear of debris
- Prune plants as needed for airflow and yield
- Keep your plants watered
- Feed the soil regularly to keep it healthy and happy
- Learn about potential pests in your area, work to prevent them, and manage them should they show up
- Acquire an understanding of common plant diseases and take necessary measures to prevent and mitigate them

Look at these tasks not as homework or chores, but as a way to build and foster a relationship with your garden. In the same way friendships can take effort and commitment on everyone's part to thrive, if you provide for your garden, it will provide for you.

Weeding

Grass growing in a carrot bed.

Weeding is an essential garden task that may seem tedious at first but will save you from major headaches down the road. If left unchecked, weeds (unwanted plants) will sprout, spread, grow, and take away vital nutrients that your vegetables and flowers need. This competition for nutrients and space can become difficult to manage once weeds have taken hold. Unfortunately, many of the common weeds we know have very long taproots. If the root itself is not removed, the weed will simply sprout back. Therefore, regular and diligent weeding is necessary to keep unwanted plants from taking hold.

A few tips on removing weeds:

- The best time to weed is when the soil is moist following rainfall or after watering.

- Your hands are your best tools, but you can certainly use a Hori Hori knife or hand hoe for those stubborn weeds and their thick roots.

- A stirrup hoe is a very useful tool that allows you to weed while standing up. Note, however, that it does not remove the root.

Learn how to identify plants by their shape, their color, and the smell of their leaves. A weed that pops up in your garden is only a weed if you don't want it there. Otherwise, it's a volunteer plant. I see volunteer plants as a bonus. I didn't have to start them, nurture them, or buy them.

Mulching your garden beds is not only beneficial from a soil protection and erosion perspective, it also helps suppress weeds by blocking out access to light and smothering them. Unsprayed straw mulch is a good option and will not disintegrate quickly. I have used straw mulch on my allotment plots and at client sites. Straw mulch works great when you're unable to tend to your garden daily and keep a watchful eye for weeds.

However, from an aesthetic point of view, I do not use it in my home garden. My backyard is a dual-purpose space. It includes the garden space where I grow food and flowers, as well as a relaxing and entertaining space for lounging and dining. I find straw mulch distracting. Because I have access to my backyard daily, I can keep an eye on weeds and pull them as needed. Consider your circumstances, preferences, and the time you're willing to dedicate to the garden when choosing whether to mulch.

Landscape fabric can be used to create a physical barrier and block weeds from growing. You can pierce or burn holes in the landscape fabric for your crops. This method is widely used in commercial organic growing environments because of the sheer volume of weeds that need to be controlled. However, I do not recommend using landscape fabric in urban and suburban gardens. It can create a disconnect between the gardener and the soil. I want you to develop a relationship with your soil. Get to know it. Understand what it needs.

Your garden paths will also require diligent weeding to stay accessible and safe to use. The techniques outlined above will help, but if you're up for it, a flame weeder is a wonderfully effective and cathartic tool that can be used on paths, driveways, and other areas where weeds sprout, provided using one is safe in your area. Watching those pesky weeds wither can be quite rewarding.

There is no substitute for hard work. Be leery of special formulas and concoctions that claim to manage weeds organically.

Watering and Irrigation Systems

I don't know about you, but I enjoy watering my garden. I disconnect from the world around me and focus entirely on the task at hand. I'm lucky to live in a region that gets a considerable amount of rainwater during the growing season. Rainwater is much more beneficial than tap water for various reasons; for one, it provides bioavailable nutrients that can be used by plants. Tap water, on the other hand, can contain added fluoride and chlorine. But even with the abundant rains in my area, I still need to use tap water to irrigate my garden and keep it healthy, lush, and thriving.

When watering, there are a few things to keep in mind:

- Don't be afraid to stick your hands in the soil. The surface of your containers and garden beds may look dry, but if the soil is moist 1" (2.5cm) below the surface, you may not need to water. Overwatering can cause a host of issues, so be conservative.

- Water early in the morning when the sun is still low in the sky. Avoid watering at midday, especially on hot sunny days.

- If possible, install a rainwater barrel to collect water to use around your garden.

- When hand watering, avoid getting any plant foliage unnecessarily wet. Water the soil surface directly. This helps reduce the risk of fungal issues (more on this later in the chapter).

- Using a hose attachment or a wand with a "shower" setting will evenly distribute water on the soil surface and not cause soil disturbance or splash back. More on why we want to avoid splash back later in this chapter.

One of my favorite ways to irrigate my urban garden is using a simple, affordable, and effective drip irrigation system. These systems, when tied to a timer, can be a lifesaver for when you're away from your garden for several days, like on vacation or work trips. They are customizable and offer home gardeners a plethora of emitter options, sprayers, misters, soaker hoses, and more. I not only use drip irrigation in my raised beds but have set the system up so that I can also water my containers and gutters automatically.

The downside of a drip irrigation system is that any water remaining in it can freeze during the winter months, causing pipes and fitting to crack. The upside? They are quite easy to repair and replace in the spring as the system is mostly aboveground.

 Scan the QR code to watch a video of my drip irrigation setup.

If you live in a very cold region and/or have a large garden to irrigate, consider hiring a landscape or irrigation professional to set up a permanent system with piping running below ground. Professional systems can also be purged in the fall to prevent the water freeze/thaw cycles that can cause the equipment to fail.

That being said, I don't recommend that a new gardener set up an irrigation system right away. Get to know your garden first. Develop an understanding of what your soil and plants need. Familiarize yourself with how container plants react at the height of summer. Manual irrigation will allow you to stop and observe your plants. This will be critical to successfully managing pests and diseases, as outlined later in the chapter.

If you live in a region with water usage restrictions, consider installing a rainwater collection system. Rain barrels are the easiest and most affordable way to collect rainwater from your home's roof by simply diverting a downspout. By elevating the rain barrel on wooden legs or cinderblocks, you are then able to use the spigot at the bottom of the tank to fill a watering can. There are more expensive systems like permanent cistern installations which require pumps and electricity. Consult with your municipality. Many cities and towns are now offering programs and discounts on rainwater collection systems.

Feeding the Soil

We ask quite a bit of our soil. As plants grow, they take in and use vital nutrients from the soil and growing media. Nutrients are not infinite, and it is our job as organic gardeners to help replenish the soil. This is why I tend to focus on feeding the soil rather than feeding the plants. This topic and its associated science could fill an entire book. I will highlight key elements and tips that home gardeners can apply practically in their gardens.

My preference is to always use organic fertilizers that focus on supporting the soil and the living things within it. By feeding the soil, we are feeding the worms and other organisms that will create the nutrients needed by our plants. For the home gardener, the available options can seem daunting. However, as more home gardeners embrace organic and regenerative practices, the marketplace is responding, so there is no shortage of products to choose from.

Organic fertilizers will often be labeled with an NPK rating. As outlined in the Fundamentals of Soil chapter, each letter of the NPK rating represents one of the primary macronutrients used by plants—

nitrogen (N), phosphorous (P), and potassium (K). Many countries have standardized the ordering of these numbers. The numbers themselves refer to the ratio or proportion of each element in the product.

These macronutrients play a critical role in overall plant health. Without getting too deep into the science, try to remember that nitrogen (N) is for leaf growth, phosphorous (P) is for root development, and potassium (K) is for overall plant health and immunity. This will help you determine the right fertilizer to use based on the specific crop.

Organic fertilizers typically need soil organisms to break them down into a form that can be used by plants. This goes back to the concept of feeding your soil rather than feeding your plants. This gradual release via organic processes is important because the plants end up using what they need. Chemical fertilizers, on the other hand, are formulated to give plants a big dose of ready-to-use elements. This can cause your plants to burn (chemical burn) and does absolutely nothing to support soil biology.

Selecting the Right Formulation

Although balanced or "all-in-one" organic fertilizers are available on the market, I prefer to tailor my approach and consider each plant's requirements.

Fruiting crops like tomatoes, peppers, and eggplants will benefit from a product with a higher concentration of phosphorous (P) and potassium (K) than nitrogen (N), since these macronutrients support flowering/fruiting and overall plant health.

Leafy green plants like lettuces, brassicas, and Asian greens will benefit from an organic fertilizer with a higher percentage of nitrogen (N) as this macronutrient will support the production of foliage, which is what we want when the focus is on producing lush and juicy leafy greens.

Longer-season root crops like potatoes and carrots should be fertilized with an organic fertilizer with very little to no nitrogen (N) and a much higher proportion of phosphorus (P), which promotes root growth.

If you followed the garden bed and container amendment recommendations outlined in the Fundamentals of Soil chapter, your raised bed or in-ground garden should not require frequent fertilization. I will generally fertilize once every 4 to 6 weeks throughout the season starting when the weather warms up in June. If I amended properly in early spring, I shouldn't need to fertilize right away.

Another tip is to keep an eye on your plants. This is important for many reasons, as I will outline in the pest and disease sections of this chapter. Nutrient deficiencies will become apparent to you if you spot stunted plants, leaf drop, or discoloration. The challenge is that these symptoms can also mean other things. My recommendation is to focus on building your soil up, supporting it, and feeding it. By focusing on your soil, you'll grow healthy and resilient plants.

Fertilizing Containers

Nutrients in containers will become depleted at a much faster rate than those in a raised bed or an in-ground garden. This is because containers are enclosed vessels with very little organic matter and biological activity in the soil to break it down and create bioavailable nutrients for the plants. This is evident by the lack of earthworms in a typical container. Therefore, containers need to be fertilized throughout the growing season, especially if you're using them to grow intensively or if you're growing heavy feeders like tomatoes and peppers.

When selecting an organic fertilizer formulation for containers, I use the same thought process outlined for in-ground and raised bed gardens above. I consider the plant's specific needs rather than using a generic all-in-one approach. However, because container nutrients deplete at a faster rate, I feed every 3 to 4 weeks. This also applies to nontraditional types of containers like grow towers and gutters.

If you are using a quality organic container mix in your planters, grow bags, and pots, then it should already come preloaded with slow-release organic fertilizer. Check the packaging and manufacturer website for more information. Many brands will claim that the mix will continuously feed for several months, but I still feed my containers since there's no way to know if the nutrients have become depleted without running a lab test.

Identifying and Managing Pests

Organic gardening brings with it many challenges and issues as far as dealing with pests. When we choose to garden organically and regeneratively, we make a vow to ourselves and the ecosystem around us not to use harmful pesticides and inhumane practices. The reason we garden organically is because we care about the environment around us and want to foster ecologically balanced gardens that not only support our personal needs but do minimal harm to wildlife in the process.

However, there are situations where a nuanced approach is needed. In situations where pest pressure is so high that it could damage property or human health, further action is required. For example, if a family of raccoons invades your attic, you will have to take action. In situations such as these, it is important to understand what your local regulations and options are. Consult with local experts.

When you start viewing the world with an ecological lens, you'll find that balance can be achieved and maintained. In this chapter, we will cover the most common garden pests, from the smallest aphid all the way up to humans. Yes, humans are destructive creatures in many respects and often the most difficult to manage.

But first, here's a rundown of common terms and products that I will refer to throughout this section.

OMRI: Organic Materials Review Institute is an organization that supports organic integrity by developing clear guidelines about materials so that producers and the general public know which products are appropriate for organic gardening uses. Often, a product will be labeled as OMRI Listed®, meaning that it is designated as safe to use in organic farming and gardening.

Neem Oil: Pressed from the seeds of the *Azadirachta indica* tree, an evergreen tree indigenous to the Indian subcontinent, neem oil is a commonly used product listed as safe for organic gardening practices by bodies such as OMRI. Many claims have been made about neem oil and it is said to have many good qualities (e.g., fungicide, insecticide, miticide). It is important to note that neem oil is not approved for horticultural applications in every jurisdiction. For example, in Canada, neem oil is currently available for purchase and use in health and beauty products, but not for horticultural use.

Diatomaceous Earth (DE): This is made of the fossilized remains of diatoms (aquatic organisms) that accumulated over millennia in freshwater lakes. This product can be an effective way to control beetles, ants, and other hard-shelled pests. Considered a "mechanical" insecticide, when an insect comes into contact with it, its sharp edges cut the insect's exoskeleton and create wounds that let body fluids escape. DE has many applications that range from use in pools to food, and it is available at varying grade levels. I recommend using food-grade DE. It is recommended to use a mask or respirator when applying DE as the particles may irritate nasal passages and lungs.

Bacillus thuringiensis (Bt): A soil-dwelling bacterium commonly used as a biological pesticide, Bt is effective at managing a range of pests. When ingested by a caterpillar, the bacteria produce proteins that paralyze the caterpillar's digestive system, causing them to stop feeding and eventually die.

Insecticidal Soap: These products made with potassium salts of fatty acids can help manage certain soft-bodied pests like aphids. Insecticidal soap does not harm plant matter, but as with any commercial product, it is important to use it as directed and ensure that it is OMRI Listed®.

Row Cover: This refers to cloth, fabric, plastic, or fiber material used to cover garden beds. The term row cover can be a catch-all term that includes polyethylene (poly) material, insect barrier, shade cloths, or frost cover.

Low Tunnel: A tunnel that is built on top of a raised bed or in-ground bed that consists of hoops, clamps, and row cover. Low tunnels are not meant to be big enough to crawl through or walk under. Poly-tunnels generally refer to larger greenhouse-like structures. A gardener can create different environments to meet a range of needs using different row cover materials. By selecting and deploying the appropriate material as a cover, it is possible to regulate various stresses on your plants. You can protect your crops from damaging pests with an insect barrier. By using poly or plastic sheeting, you can create a miniature greenhouse where you can control the temperature. And you can also shield crops from damaging temperatures by employing frost cover.

Chicken Wire / Hardware Cloth: As the name suggests, chicken wire is used to create fencing or enclosures for chickens. However, this material can be used in myriad ways to protect crops from pests. Hardware cloth is similar to chicken wire, but with smaller openings and a more rigid structure.

Organza Bags: These are bags typically used for wedding favors and gifts (think candy-covered almonds). However, organza bags are also a great way to protect your fruits and vegetables in the garden. They come in a range of sizes; smaller bags can be used to protect individual fruits, while larger bags can be used for clusters like cherry tomatoes.

Before I run down a fairly extensive list of pests and recommended management practices, I'd like to cover some high-level practices that will help you with your pest management and prevention activities.

- **Be present.** Walk around your garden, observe, and turn leaves over. Being present is one of the main ways to identify (and hopefully remedy or prevent) major infestations or issues.

- **"Pest-free" is not attainable.** An organic, ecological garden will always have pests. That's a certainty. Our role as organic gardeners is to foster a balanced environment and support the growth of healthy resilient plants that can withstand some pest pressure.

- **Not all bugs are equal.** Learn how to identify pests and understand their role in the garden. Many insects are beneficial (including parasitoids, predators, and pollinators) and can help you achieve balance in the garden. Understand the difference between native and invasive species. An invasive pest in one part of the world could be considered a native and beneficial species in another.

- **Err on the side of caution.** Even if a product is marked as safe for organic use, it doesn't mean that it should be used indiscriminately. Organic pesticides are still pesticides and may be damaging to beneficial insects. Only reach for them if all other management methods have failed. Be conservative and extremely targeted with their application.

Pests

Aphids: Aphids are small sap-sucking insects that come in a variety of colors. You'll find them on many crops including greens, brassicas, roses, and more. They tend to cause plant leaves to curl. If you spot curled leaves, take a proactive approach and inspect further. In large quantities, aphids can cause significant plant stress, especially if the aphids are congregating around growth points. The best course of action is to use a hose and blast them off. Another great way to control aphids is to attract lady beetles (ladybugs) to your garden; you can also purchase dormant ladybugs and release them in the garden. Ladybugs, and even more so ladybug larvae, will feast on aphids. They are a great beneficial insect to attract to your garden. You can also use an organic insecticide like neem oil or insecticidal soap if you have an infestation. If you do spot aphids on your plants, wait a day or two before trying to manage them. Their presence may attract beneficial insects.

Hornworms: These are large green caterpillars, the larvae of the *Manduca sexta* or *Manduca*

quinquemaculata moths. The larvae feed on tomato foliage and can decimate a plant if left unchecked. The challenge is spotting them in the first place since they camouflage themselves well. You will know that they are lurking in your tomato vines by the excrement they leave behind; clumps of excrement the size of pencil erasers are a telltale sign. Once you locate a hornworm, you can either dispose of it or do what I do and relocate it to another part of the garden with a trap crop (another tomato vine). If you're not willing to bring it to its demise, a parasitic braconid wasp might. These wasps (which are beneficial insects) lay eggs in the bodies of hornworms. The wasp larvae feed internally on the hornworm until they emerge and spin white cocoons on the bodies of the hornworm. When you see one, it is best to let it be as it will die soon and many beneficial wasps will be born. Cut off the leaf on which a parasitized caterpillar is sitting and relocate it somewhere so that the wasps can hatch safely.

Japanese Beetles: Green and copper oval-shaped

beetles, they are pervasive, destructive pests. They begin their life cycle as grubs in the ground, then they emerge as beetles that shimmer in the sun. They reproduce ferociously and the cycle continues. In North America, they are an invasive species that is a major nuisance, one that requires active management in the home garden. Picking them off by hand is essential to help decrease the population. This is best done in the morning when they are not as active. Arm yourself with a jar of soapy water and hand-pick or flick them into the jar.

Some recommend the use of beneficial nematodes as a way to control this pest in the grub stage. However, in urban and suburban gardens, this technique is not very helpful because these beetles can travel and you would need to apply beneficial nematodes in a wide radius. Beware of using pheromone traps that are marketed to manage this pest. You may end up attracting your neighborhood's Japanese beetle population to your own garden.

Flea Beetles: Small, jumping insects that are barely visible, flea beetles feed on foliage, leaving small, irregular holes all over the leaves. They are difficult to control organically but are not generally a problem; healthy plants tend not to be negatively impacted. Flea beetles will overwinter in dead plant matter left on the surface of the soil. Garden hygiene and the removal of dead and diseased plant matter will help control their populations. They are active in spring, which is when we typically set out seedlings. To protect tender and immature seedlings from flea beetle pressure, cover your seedlings with an insect barrier. For larger infestations, DE can be applied to plant foliage. Reapply DE after a rainfall.

Cabbage Butterfly: Commonly referred to as cabbage moths, these little white butterflies are a regular sight in many parts of the world. They look innocent enough but can be incredibly destructive. They lay small white eggs, predominantly on crops in the Brassica genus (e.g., cabbage, broccoli, and kale) and typically on the underside of leaves. Eggs hatch into green larvae that feed on the leaves. They are difficult to identify because they camouflage quite well and remain on the underside of leaves for several days. The most organic way to manage them is to prevent the butterflies from laying eggs in the first place by deploying row cover. Alternatively, you can check the underside of brassica leaves regularly and remove eggs before they hatch. In larger gardens where row cover is not an option, Bt can be used to manage them.

Leaf Miner: The larval stage of a moth, sawfly, fly, or beetle, a leaf miner is destructive because it will hatch on the underside of a leaf and burrow (or mine) between the leaf's outer membranes, leaving behind distinctive irregular streaks. The only way to prevent this is to stop the adult insect from laying its eggs in the first place. This can be done by deploying row cover. Proactively checking your plants for tiny white egg clusters (and rubbing them off with your fingers) also helps catch them before they hatch and burrow into your beet greens, chard, and spinach. If you find leaves that are already infested with leaf miner, carefully prune and discard them to prevent further infestation.

Cucumber Beetles: These are yellow and black beetles that are striped or dotted. As the name suggests, they attack cucumbers and other members of the cucurbit family (e.g., squash, zucchini, and melons). They are problematic because not only do they eat foliage and flowers, but they can also transmit diseases such as bacterial wilt. In the organic garden, preventing them from showing up is no easy task. Covering with an insect barrier is not a viable option since this will prevent pollinators from visiting your cucurbit flowers and pollinating them. Hand-picking or dropping the beetles into soapy water is the only way to help reduce their population and mitigate the risk of disease. If their numbers are significant and you have a major outbreak on your hands, consider applying DE on the leaves. Avoid applying DE to flowers.

Squash Bugs: As the name suggests, these prehistoric-looking insects prefer squash plants and other members of the cucurbit family (e.g., zucchini, cucumber, and melons). They are often confused with stink bugs because with their shield-like exoskeletons, they look quite similar. Squash bugs live underground and will reproduce on the stems and leaves of cucurbits. You can easily tell if they are present by the clusters of copper-colored eggs they lay on the underside of squash leaves. Organically speaking, they are difficult to control. Because they live underground, crop rotation can help mitigate their damage. Eggs should be removed quickly. They are quite stubborn and difficult to remove with your fingers. The easiest way to remove them is to wrap duct tape around your fingers with the sticky side facing out. The eggs will stick to the duct tape glue, but be careful not to cause damage to plant foliage. Hand-picking the bugs off is possible, but they tend to scurry away. For larger infestations, DE can be applied to the squash stems and around the base of the plant. Avoid applying DE to flowers.

Slugs and Snails: Part of the gastropod *mollusca* family, slugs (no shell) and snails (with shell) are some of the most common garden pests in the world. They feed on a range of plants but tend to go after tender greens like lettuce, young plant stems, and even strawberries. Slugs and snails thrive in moist and humid conditions and are more prevalent in wetter parts of the world. While we can't control our climate, we can control when and how we add more moisture to our gardens. Avoid watering in the evening as excess water won't have

an opportunity to evaporate or dry off, creating favorable conditions for these pests. Allow the surface of your soil to dry out slightly between watering sessions. Remove plant debris from the surface of your soil, and space out your planters and containers so that there's room for air to circulate. Manually picking them off your plants, though quite disgusting, is one way to manage these pests. Beer traps are a popular method of trapping slugs and other pests in the garden. Fill cups or small deli containers with an inch or two of beer and sink them into the soil so that the rims of the cups/containers are level with the soil. Be sure to not disturb plants or root structures in the process. DE can also be used in the case of large infestations.

Squash Vine Borer: As with many other garden pests, the larval stage of this moth can inflict serious damage to summer and winter squash and zucchini plants. The moth lays its eggs at the base of the squash stem. Once the egg hatches, the larva burrows into the hollow stem of the plant, where it continues to grow. Although the vines may continue to grow and produce fruit, squash vine borers can weaken plants, making them more susceptible to damage from other pests or diseases.

Observational skills are key in finding unhatched eggs as well as identifying damage. One telltale sign that your vines are infected is yellow or orange frass (insect droppings resembling sawdust in texture) appearing on the squash vines and stems. More severe damage can even include vines splitting open. In the organic garden, prevention is key to success. Using a row cover will help prevent the moth from laying its eggs in the first place. Note that with this method, you will have to actively hand-pollinate the squash flowers. In severe cases, you may have to use box cutters to cut open the stems and physically remove the larvae. Another technique involves locating the larvae and using a pin to puncture them while they are still inside the vine. To avoid the need for these drastic measures, it is best to be vigilant and keep a lookout for eggs before they hatch.

Rats, Mice, and Other Rodents: Rodents are problematic and destructive for several reasons. Not only do they pick and gnaw at fruits, but they will also pull freshly transplanted seedlings from the ground and burrow in both raised and in-ground beds, causing a mess and disturbing delicate root structures. When building new raised beds, it is imperative to staple hardware cloth at the bottom to prevent rodents from entering from below. If rodents are a serious problem in your area, consider adding fencing around your growing area. If you must use traps, choose humane traps or use a local pest control service that is certified by your local jurisdiction. Although they are readily available, never use poison pellets. This can harm other local wildlife as well as neighborhood cats.

Squirrels: Although they are rodents and cause damage similar to what rats, mice, and voles do, squirrels deserve their own category. They are destructive and problematic for anyone living in urban areas with mature trees. There isn't much an organic gardener can do to deter them since they can climb, jump, and get anywhere they like. Physical barriers are a good deterrent. More aggressive methods include motion-activated water sprayers. These devices work because over time, they condition the animals not to visit your garden. Organza bags can be used to protect prized crops and fruits. They aren't 100% effective against squirrels but can certainly help.

Raccoons: Much like squirrels, raccoons can climb and get anywhere they please. In urban centers, they don't generally go after fruits and vegetables in your garden because they prefer foraging in household garbage. They tend to dig up containers and garden beds looking for grubs and other insects, seeds, and nuts.

Birds: Our winged friends will peck at fruits and vegetables for their water content. Including a bird bath is a good way to provide them with access to water and keep them away from your prized tomatoes. Protecting freshly planted seedlings with row cover until they are established is also good practice since birds can dislodge seedlings in your garden and pick at them.

Humans: Some may argue humans are the most destructive animal to inhabit the earth. Chemical herbicide, pesticide, and fertilizer use is rampant not only in rural areas but also within urban centers. For example, a neighbor may spray their lawn with herbicide. Herbicide spray can travel, especially on a windy day, and may land in your organic garden. Strike up a conversation with your neighbors and ask them to warn you the next time they plan to use these products. They may even begin to wonder why you care so much and start to question their own practices.

Identifying and Managing Disease

One of the biggest challenges an organic gardener will face is disease in the garden; it's practically a certainty. What makes this even more difficult is that many plant diseases present themselves similarly with symptoms like browning and/or yellowing of foliage. In terms of possible treatments, options are limited for the organic gardener; however, copper-based and sulfur-based fungicides can be used as directed. Neem oil is another product with fungicidal properties. Your mileage may vary with some of these products; personally, I avoid using them in my garden and prefer to focus on what I can control.

As discussed in the soil health chapter, focusing on building healthy soil will encourage healthy plants to thrive. Healthy and vigorous plants can withstand pest and disease pressure better than weaker plants. Don't overlook the importance of soil in the prevention and mitigation of disease in your edible garden.

Common sense garden hygiene practices also help reduce the chance of spreading diseases.

- **Wash equipment** like garden pots, tools, cell packs, cell trays, and seed starting equipment to prevent the spread or overwintering of disease. This can be done with a bleach solution (a 10% solution—1 part bleach to 10 parts water). You can also wash your equipment with soapy water and then wipe it down with 70% isopropyl alcohol.

- **Rotate your crops.** Avoid planting the same crop in the same location in your garden. This can be difficult in an urban setting where space is at a premium. The same concept applies to containers.

- **Mulching.** Apply mulch on your soil or growing medium to help prevent soil-borne disease splash back when watering or during heavy rains.

- **Irrigation.** Use drip irrigation or soaker hoses, or water the soil surface with extra care to avoid getting plant foliage unnecessarily wet.

- **Pruning and airflow.** Prune the lower leaves of common plants like tomatoes, peppers, and eggplants to reduce the chance of disease spread. Airflow is key to a healthy garden.

- **Be vigilant.** Observe your plants. Prune diseased leaves early and often. If a plant is looking like it is too far gone or may not recover, consider discarding it entirely.

Important note: Diseased plant matter should be discarded in the garbage and not added to your compost pile. Household compost systems rarely reach the temperatures needed to kill off plant diseases, pathogens, or weed seeds. If your city collects organic matter and yard waste, consult the requirements around what can and cannot be collected.

Early Blight: A fungal disease that affects plants in the nightshade family such as tomatoes, peppers, eggplants, and potatoes, early blight is brought on by a pathogen called *Alternaria solani*. It causes bullseye brown discoloration on leaves, stem legions, and fruit rot. The infection begins at the bottom of the plant and works its way up. The pathogen overwinters in plant material and soil. It can be spread by splashing rain, insects, and non-sanitized garden tools. Treatment includes using a copper-based fungicide. I would also recommend you prune lower leaves to limit splash back, keep your soil mulched, give your plants ample room to breathe, use soaker hoses or drip irrigation, and rotate your planting areas.

Late Blight: Like early blight, late blight is a fungal disease that also affects plants in the nightshade family. It is caused by *Phytophthora infestans* and generally occurs late in the growing season. This disease starts at the lower part of the plant and works its way up, appearing as gray/green spots on leaves and then starts producing white fungal growths. Late blight does not overwinter but can be transmitted in the air by flying insects and from previously infested nursery seedlings. Treatment options for late blight are similar to those for early blight: using a copper-based fungicide, pruning lower leaves to avoid splash back, keeping your soil mulched, giving your plants ample room to breathe, using soaker hoses or drip irrigation, and rotating your planting areas.

Southern Blight: Southern blight is another fungal disease primarily affecting plants in the nightshade family, as well as a host of other crops. Caused by the fungus *Sclerotium rolfsii*, the earliest visible symptoms are small brown lesions on the stem as well as the water-soaked appearance of lower leaves. As the disease progresses, white cotton-like growths appear on the stems near the soil line (these are mycelial bodies—the vegetative part of a fungus). Leaves will yellow, turn brown, and fall. The disease overwinters in the soil as sclerotia, a compact mass of hardened fungal mycelium. This is a difficult disease to manage.

Bacterial Wilt: As the name suggests, this is a bacterial disease. Several pathogens fall under the umbrella term bacterial wilt. *Bacterium R. solanacearum* affects members of the nightshade family (e.g., tomatoes, peppers, and eggplants). *Bacterium Erwinia tracheiphila* affects members of the cucurbit family (e.g., squash, zucchini, and pumpkins). The initial stages of the disease show up as the wilted appearance of the youngest leaves. Eventually, the entire plant wilts and dies. There is no treatment for bacterial wilt, and the best ways to prevent it are to employ crop rotation, use sterilized gardening tools, mulch your soil, and hand-pick off pests that are known to carry this disease, such as cucumber beetles.

Septoria Leaf Spot: Caused by the fungus *Septoria lycopersici*, Septoria leaf spot is a fungal disease that affects tomatoes. This is a very destructive disease and is prevalent in areas known for wet, humid summers. This disease presents itself as small, round spots on the lowest leaves; spots are brown on the edges and tan/white in the centers. Septoria overwinters in the soil and can be transmitted to plants via splash back. No treatment is available. Prevention is the best defense.

Powdery Mildew: Powdery mildew affects a wide range of plants, including tomatoes, squash, and cucumbers. This is a fungal disease caused by *Podosphaera xanthii* and shows up as a white powdery substance on plant foliage. It thrives in dry and warm areas (which is unusual, because we expect diseases to spread in damp conditions). As it spreads, it prevents the plants from thriving, thus reducing the chances of survival and good yields. Powdery mildew is difficult to cure, but you can help reduce the speed at which it spreads by pruning affected foliage and applying sulfur or copper-based fungicides. Breeders are now creating hybrid plants that offer some resistance to powdery mildew.

Mosaic Virus: Viral diseases are difficult to diagnose and affect a range of crops like tomatoes, squash, cauliflower, and cucumbers. This condition shows up as leaves mottled with yellow, white, and light or dark green spots or streaks. Plants become stunted and exhibit abnormal growth patterns. As with other viral diseases, nothing can be done to save the plant. Remove and discard in the garbage (not in the compost pile). Sanitize equipment.

Bacterial Leaf Spot: This disease caused by the *Xanthomonas* and *Pseudomonas* families of bacteria presents itself as small brown spots with a yellow edge. These bacteria spread in wet and cool conditions and can be passed from plant to plant by overhead watering.

The world of plant disease, identification, and treatment is vast and can be quite daunting for the home gardener. My advice is to practice good and consistent garden hygiene, observe your plants, and take action quickly to reduce the chance of disease spread. If you have a major outbreak, seek professional help from a local plant expert or a plant nursery you trust.

Pruning and Pinching

Pruning plants in the edible garden is done for a multitude of reasons. Pruning away and discarding diseased plant matter is probably the main reason why you would want to actively prune. Another reason is to encourage proper airflow. Pruning is also performed to encourage a vining crop to grow in a certain formation, direction, or pattern.

It is critical to understand a crop's growth habits before reaching for the pruners because you can potentially cut away the growth tip, which may spell disaster for the plant in question. Keen observation is important, as stated earlier.

A few tips on successful pruning:

- Always use clean pruners or shears; disinfect them regularly to avoid spreading disease.

- Avoid pruning during or after rainfall. Allow your plants to dry before proceeding since water can help spread disease.

- Don't be afraid to cut away any yellowing or brown foliage. Yellowing foliage can mean many things, but essentially that foliage is dead or dying and is no longer useful to the plant.

- If leaves are touching the soil surface (especially with crops from the nightshade family), cut them off.

- No diseased plant matter should be composted. When in doubt, throw it out (in the garbage).

Special Consideration—Tomatoes: Growing indeterminate tomato varieties may require that you actively prune away suckers, the new vining growth tips that emerge from the connection point between a leaf and the main stem. If left unchecked, these suckers will grow into fruiting branches. In an urban gardening situation where crops are grown intensively, I recommend actively pruning away these suckers before they get too large. Training your plants to only have one or two main stems will yield a better crop because the plants will focus their energy. Note that if you have ample space and can dedicate more room to each tomato plant, you do not need to be as diligent with pruning suckers.

Pinching, on the other hand, is the active pruning of the growing tip of a crop to encourage it to branch out. Certain crops benefit greatly from pinching. These include many herbs like basil, thyme, sage, and rosemary. Regular harvesting of herbs encourages the plants to grow side shoots and to grow bigger and bushier. Other crops like dahlias, zinnias, and snapdragons also benefit from pinching and end up producing more flower stems to harvest and enjoy. Certain schools of thought also encourage pinching of cucurbits like cucumbers and squash, however, I do not recommend this. In my years of gardening experience, I have never had to actively pinch cucurbits and they have gone on to produce beautifully.

Chapter 10

Season Extension and Winterization

Extending the Growing Season

In areas where the growing season is short, deploying tools such as low tunnels and cold frames can potentially add several weeks or even months to your growing season.

As described earlier, a low tunnel is a system comprised of hoops and a cover installed over a raised bed or in-ground garden bed. The cover material can be swapped out depending on the need at a given time. In the context of extending the growing season, we want to create a miniature greenhouse by deploying a polyethylene (poly) material. This plastic material creates a sealed environment around your crops, amplifying the sun's rays within and warming up the air. This allows your crops to continue to grow in favorable conditions, even though the air temperature outside the low tunnel may be near or below freezing. This can be combined with a frost cloth or barrier applied right above the crops to help retain warmth throughout the night when the sun is not shining.

A cold frame works in a similar fashion but is typically constructed from wood or composite sides and a plexiglass roof. Cold frames work well for crops that are low to the ground like lettuce, carrots, and spinach.

In my opinion, extending the growing season with low tunnels or cold frames is an advanced topic. If you are a beginner gardener, I would suggest waiting a season or two before attempting to use season extenders. They take some practice and work better in some regions than others.

For an in-depth look at my low tunnel system, I encourage you to scan the QR code.

Winterization

The days are getting shorter and the autumn air is crisp. As winter approaches, there are some important tasks a gardener needs to address.

For Those in Regions That Experience Frost

Warm-weather crops like tomatoes, peppers, and eggplants will gladly keep growing and flowering into the cool autumn months, though at a slower pace. The challenge is that none of these flowers will have a chance to set fruit and mature before the plants die back at first frost. I recommend topping your tomato plants about 4 weeks before your first expected frost date. This practice is quite simple and involves pruning or cutting away the growth tips of your tomato vines. This allows the vines to focus on ripening existing fruit rather than setting new fruit. A similar approach can be taken with cucumbers, melons, winter squash, and other vining crops.

With peppers and eggplants, I recommend disbudding your plants 4 weeks before your first frost. The process involves actively removing any new flowers and small fruit that won't have a chance to mature in time. You will have to repeat this process a few times. Any winter squash or pumpkins you currently have on the vine should be harvested before a hard frost is expected since it could potentially damage the fruit. Keep an eye on the forecast and take necessary action. Winter squash and pumpkin fruits may survive a light frost but the vines themselves will be affected.

If frost is expected earlier than usual, you can use frost cloth to protect sensitive crops through the night. Container-grown crops can be brought into a garage or shed for shelter.

When the weather finally takes a chilly turn and there's no reasonable way to keep your warm-weather crops going in optimal growing conditions, snip all plants down to the soil surface. Discard any diseased, yellow, or dry plant matter and compost whatever looks healthy. Personally, I discard tomato, pepper, eggplant, and basil plants at the end of the season rather than compost them because they will most probably have been affected by blight, mildew, and a host of other issues. Avoid pulling the root ball. In a no-till garden, the roots remain in the soil and are allowed to decompose slowly, providing food for soil organisms. Remove any fallen fruit or leaves from the surface of the soil to reduce the likelihood of volunteer plants in the spring and the overwintering of diseased plant matter.

The same principle applies to containers. Cut your plants down to the growing medium surface. Leave the root balls intact. They will decompose slowly over the winter months. Containers can be stacked against a fence or wall or moved into a sheltered space like a shed or garage. Terracotta and plastic containers may require careful insulation since they tend to crack as the growing medium freezes and thaws throughout the winter months.

As the weather gets colder, some crops may remain in the ground. These include cool-weather crops and crops that can overwinter (depending on your zone and microclimate). Examples include carrots, onions, and kale. In fact, many of these crops will taste better once they have experienced a frost. Brassicas that have not yet fully matured may also remain in the ground. Depending on the weather conditions, they may continue to grow or they may slow down altogether. If so inclined, you can use season extenders to keep your cool-weather crops cozy and comfortable until you need to harvest them.

A note on potted perennial herbs: In order to ensure that your potted perennial herbs survive winter and come back next year, you might need to take additional precautions to insulate or protect them. If left unprotected, potted herbs can experience freeze/thaw cycles and oversaturation of the growing medium from rain and snow melt, which can lead to rotting.

Dig holes in your garden or raised beds and drop the pots into the ground so that the tops of the pots are level with the soil line. A thick layer of mulch will provide further insulation. In the spring, when the soil thaws, you can simply take the pot out, and the perennial herbs should have survived. Alternatively, you can stack your perennial herb pots in a sheltered and dry location that is blocked from the blistering winter wind (I like to stack them against the side wall of my house). You can also cover the pots with frost cloth and/or leaf or straw mulch for further insulation.

For Those in Regions That Don't Experience Frost

If you reside in zone 10 or higher, luckily for you, many of the concerns listed above do not apply. However, your summer crops will eventually succumb to disease or simply old age. Prune at the base and discard or compost as outlined above. At that point, based on your zone and climate, you can decide to switch to cool-weather crops or consider growing a cover crop. Cover crops are used to increase soil fertility in the off-season. By growing a cover crop such as grasses or legumes, you are helping give back to your soil after it has given you so much throughout the growing season.

Feed your soil, and it will feed your soul.

Glossary of Terms

The amount of unfamiliar terminology in the gardening space can be overwhelming, especially for new gardeners. Here is a list of common terms and brief definitions for them. These terms are covered in much greater detail in Chapters 4–10. Refer to the Index to look up page numbers where these terms are used and/or described.

Bacillus thuringiensis (Bt): A soil-dwelling bacterium commonly used as a biological pesticide.

Blanching (Cauliflower): The act of physically covering the developing cauliflower head from the sun to avoid discoloration.

Bolting: Also referred to as going to flower or going to seed, this term describes what happens when crops that are not typically cultivated for their flowers or seeds send out a flower stalk either as the weather warms up or under stress. When this occurs, the plants typically become unappetizing and bitter.

Certified Organic seeds: As the name suggests, seeds that include this label are certified by an accredited certifying agency in the jurisdiction where they are produced and/or sold.

Compost: One of the best sources of organic matter, it is created by decomposing organic matter like food waste into simpler organic and inorganic compounds.

Damping off: Soil-borne fungal disease that affects new seedlings and is characterized by the rotting of tender stems at or below the soil line. There is no cure or corrective action to be taken.

Days to Maturity (DTM): Approximate number of days it will take a crop to be ready for harvest after it has been transplanted into the ground under ideal conditions.

Determinate (also referred to as bush or patio): Crop varieties that are bred to remain compact rather than vining uncontrollably like indeterminate varieties.

Diatomaceous Earth (DE): The fossilized remains of diatoms (aquatic organisms) that have accumulated over millennia in freshwater lakes. This product can be an effective way to control beetles, ants, and other hard-shelled pests.

Direct Sow or Direct Seed: These terms refer to seeds that prefer to be planted directly into the garden or directly seeding a crop in the garden.

Germination rate: The rate at which a seed batch will germinate. For example, a 95% germination rate indicates that out of 100 seeds sown, 95 will germinate.

Hardiness Zone: Numbered zones that include regions with similar minimum average annual temperatures. Primarily used to quantify the survivability of perennial plants through winter.

Heirloom seeds: "Old World" open-pollinated varieties that have existed for many years, passed down from one generation of gardeners and farmers to the next.

Hybrid seeds: Hybrids are varieties that have been specifically bred for certain traits, including disease resistance, fruit shape, color, growth habit, high yield, and other characteristics.

Indeterminate (also referred to as vining): Describes crop varieties that grow in a vining pattern. They are considered indeterminate because under the right conditions, they can continue to grow to an undetermined length or height.

Insecticidal soaps: These products made with potassium salts of fatty acids can help manage certain soft-bodied pests like aphids.

Low tunnel: A tunnel that is built on top of a raised bed or an in-ground bed that consists of hoops, clamps, and row cover.

OMRI: Organic Materials Review Institute, an organization that supports organic integrity by developing clear guidelines about materials so that producers and the general public know which products are appropriate for organic gardening uses.

Open-pollinated seeds: Open-pollination or open-pollinated refers to seeds that will generally breed true to type either by birds, insects, wind, or even humans.

Manure: Composted animal waste, usually from sheep, cows, or horses.

Mulch: An organic product such as straw or compost used to protect bare soil from erosion, regulate temperature fluctuations, and suppress weeds.

Neem Oil: Pressed from the seeds of the Azadirachta indica tree, an evergreen tree in the Indian subcontinent, neem oil is an organic pest and disease management product listed as safe for use by bodies such as OMRI.

Potting mix (sometimes called potting soil): A growing medium formulated specifically for containers.

Row cover: Cloth, fabric, plastic, or fiber material used to cover garden beds. The term row cover can be a catch-all term that includes polyethylene (poly) material, insect barrier, shade cloths, or frost cover.

Seed starting mix: As the name suggests, it is a soilless product similar to potting mix that is used for seed starting projects.

Triple mix (a.k.a. 3-way mix): A commercially packaged product that typically contains peat moss, compost, and topsoil.

Worm Castings: An organic form of fertilizer or soil amender generated through vermicomposting.

Resources

Listed here are my preferred suppliers for all my home gardening needs. The sources noted here are based in North America.

Unfortunately, I do not have experience sourcing products in Europe, Australia, or Asia. My recommendation is to seek out organic amendment options and research the suppliers so that you can be confident in your purchase.

Seed, Bulb, and Tuber Vendors

Johnny's Selected Seeds
johnnyseeds.com
US-based seed and tool supplier catering to farmers and home gardeners. Ships internationally.

West Coast Seeds
westcoastseeds.com
Canada-based seed, tuber, and bulb supplier. Ships to both USA and Canada.

Unicorn Blooms
unicornblooms.com
Supplier of quality bulbs, corms, and tubers.

Garden Suppliers

Lee Valley Tools
leevalley.com
Canada-based supplier of high-end tools and garden supplies.

Gardener's Supply Company
gardeners.com
US-based garden tool and equipment supplier.

Organic Amendments and Fertilizer Sources

Gaia Green Organics
gaiagreen.com
Canada-based supplier of high-quality organic amendments. Products are also available in the USA.

Neptune's Harvest
neptunesharvest.com
US-based supplier of liquid organic fertilizers. Select products are also available in Canada.

Espoma
espoma.com
US-based supplier of organic amendments and growing media.

Acknowledgments

First and foremost, a special thank you to Laura Wright, who graciously wrote the foreword for my book. I am constantly inspired by your approach to food, sustainability, and work ethic. Thank you to Deanna Talerico, Afrim Pristine, and Niki Irving for your endorsements and kind words.

Thank you to Heather and Reverie Farm for allowing me to come into your space and grow an abundant and beautiful garden. Thank you to my friend Roberto for helping me craft the cocktail menu. Thank you to Charlene for allowing me to photograph in your beautiful kitchen. Thank you to my business partner Melissa for your support. Infinite gratitude to my father for sparking my gardening interest and passion, and to my amazing mother for inspiring me. I love you both immensely.

Thank you to my family, friends, and recipe testers for your support, encouragement, and feedback throughout the book writing process.

Thank you to the entire team at Mango Publishing for this wonderful opportunity to conceptualize and create a book that encapsulates my garden-to-table philosophy. Thank you for the encouragement, feedback, and support throughout this whole process.

Thank you to my Instagram and TikTok followers, clients, blog readers, and Master Class students for your unwavering support. Thank you to *you*! My thanks to all of my readers. It's incredibly rewarding to share my passion and knowledge with the world, and I am grateful to you all.

Last but certainly not loast, thank you to my partner Bernie for keeping me fed and caffeinated throughout the writing process. Your reassurance, support, "tough love," and help throughout this journey were invaluable. I could not have done it without you.

P.S.

I truly hope that you enjoyed this book and that it motivates you to think about the endless possibilities a garden can provide, no matter whether you have a small urban balcony or a large plot of land. Growing food is a universal language that connects us all. I welcome your feedback. If you have any questions, please don't hesitate to reach out by email (luay@urbanfarmandkitchen.com) or find me on Instagram, Facebook, or TikTok.

If you enjoyed this book, I would certainly appreciate it if you could leave a review on Amazon. This is immensely important for a first-time author such as myself. Once again, thank you.

About the Author

Luay Ghafari is an urban gardener, garden educator, consultant, recipe developer, and founder of *Urban Farm and Kitchen*, a seasonal garden-to-table food blog and gardening resource. His mission is to guide and help anyone on a gardening and food-growing journey. With over a decade of intensive urban growing experience, he uses tried-and-true science-based techniques to grow abundant, healthy, and thriving gardens for himself and his clients. He is passionate about the garden-to-table movement and vegetable-forward seasonal recipes. He also teaches a garden-to-table Master Class for beginner and intermediate gardeners. He has been featured in publications like *Medium*, *Food52*, and *Toronto Life Magazine*, as well as in documentaries and is active on social media, where he shares gardening tips and seasonal recipes. Luay is based in Toronto, Canada.

QR Code Web Links

Page 19 Welcome Message
urbanfarmandkitchen.com/seed-to-table/welcome-video

Page 136 Tomato Tart Blog Post
urbanfarmandkitchen.com/tomato-and-herbed-cheese-puff-pastry-tart/

Page 140 Mutabal Blog Post
urbanfarmandkitchen.com/mutabal-roasted-eggplant-dip/

Page 144 Grilled Peach Salsa Blog Post
urbanfarmandkitchen.com/peach-tomatillo-salsa/

Page 167 Cherry Tomato Ideas Blog Post
urbanfarmandkitchen.com/what-to-do-with-all-those-cherry-tomatoes/

Page 242 Gutter Vertical Growing System
urbanfarmandkitchen.com/seed-to-table/gutter-vertical-growing-system

Page 276 Seed Starting Shelving Unit
urbanfarmandkitchen.com/seed-to-table/seed-starting-shelving-unit

Page 278 Seed Starting Process
urbanfarmandkitchen.com/seed-to-table/seed-starting-process

Page 285 Potting Up
urbanfarmandkitchen.com/seed-to-table/potting-up

Page 294 Drip Irrigation System
urbanfarmandkitchen.com/seed-to-table/drip-irrigation-system

Page 313 Low Tunnel Setup
urbanfarmandkitchen.com/seed-to-table/low-tunnel-setup

Page 322 Thank You Message
urbanfarmandkitchen.com/seed-to-table/thank-you-message

Index

yellow pear 🍐 press

Yellow Pear Press, established in 2015, publishes inspiring, charming, clever, distinctive, playful, imaginative, beautifully designed lifestyle books, cookbooks, literary fiction, notecards, and journals with a certain *joie de vivre* in both content and style. Yellow Pear Press books have been honored by the Independent Publisher Book (IPPY) Awards, National Indie Excellence Awards, Independent Press Awards, and International Book Awards. Reviews of our titles have appeared in Kirkus Reviews, Foreword Reviews, Booklist, Midwest Book Review, San Francisco Chronicle, and New York Journal of Books, among others. Yellow Pear Press joined forces with Mango Publishing in 2020, with the vision to continue publishing clever and innovative books. The fact that they're both named after fruit is a total coincidence.

We love hearing from our readers, so please stay in touch with us and follow us at:

Facebook: Mango Publishing
Twitter: @MangoPublishing
Instagram: @MangoPublishing
LinkedIn: Mango Publishing
Pinterest: Mango Publishing

Newsletter: mangopublishinggroup.com/newsletter